EUROPE IN
THE AGE OF
IMPERIALISM:
1880–1914

1, 2 Early architectural visions of imperialism. Designs for an imperial palace for the sovereigns of the British Empire and new Houses of Parliament, by J.M. Gandy, 1834 and 1836

EUROPE IN THE AGE OF IMPERIALISM 1880-1914

HEINZ GOLLWITZER

Professor of Modern Political and Social History,
Westfälische Wilhelms Universität, Münster

W · W · NORTON & COMPANY · INC · New York

Translated from the German by David Adam and Stanley Baron

First American edition 1969
This edition published by W. W. Norton & Company Inc. 1979

Printed in Great Britain by Jarrold and Sons Ltd, Norwich

ISBN 0-393-95104-9

CONTENTS

PREFACE   7

I THE IMPERIALIST AGE   9

II THE DEMOGRAPHIC   19
SITUATION AND THE
TECHNICAL REVOLUTION IN
NATURAL SCIENCE

III THE WORLD POLITICAL   31
CONSTELLATION

IV NATIONALISM; 'PAN'   41
MOVEMENTS;
EMPIRE IDEOLOGIES

V ECONOMICS IN THE AGE OF   61
IMPERIALISM

VI THE SOCIAL STRUCTURE IN   81
THE AGE OF IMPERIALISM

VII ORGANIZATIONS OF THE   101
IMPERIALIST MOVEMENT

VIII THE ANTI-IMPERIALIST 117
FRONT

IX IMPERIUM ET LIBERTAS 125

X SOCIAL IMPERIALISM 133

XI IMPERIALISM AS REFLECTED 141
IN LITERATURE AND ART

XII IMPERIALISM AND LEARNING 153

XIII IMPERIALIST 165
WELTANSCHAUUNG AND
ATTITUDES TO LIFE

XIV THE END OF AN EPOCH AND 182
ITS SIGNIFICANCE

SELECT BIBLIOGRAPHY 197

LIST OF ILLUSTRATIONS 208

INDEX 211

PREFACE

In conformity with the character of the series within whose framework it appears, this book deals with the internal history of Europe and not with diplomatic history, foreign policy or the impact of Europeans overseas. The question of whether this can be an adequate approach naturally arises the moment the catchword 'imperialism' is uttered. If ever a policy can be stamped as extroverted, if ever a policy developed tendencies of expansion and transformed them into an ideology, if ever a policy tightened the links binding the European states and the rest of the world more closely than ever before, it was imperialist policy. I do not disavow this and nothing is further from my mind than to imply a preference for the line of thought followed in this book. In writing this history I hold to a pluralistic and combinational principle. It was tempting to produce an essay oriented towards the social and historical attitudes of imperialism in Europe. There is certainly no lack of books and treatises on European colonial policies, nor of histories dealing with wars in European and overseas theatres; and the most important facts and events in this sphere also form part and parcel of the present book, but only to define an 'inner view' when grappling with the epoch between the 1880s and the First World War. The fact that American and Japanese imperialism are not discussed can only be excused by the concept of the series, which is devoted to civilization in Europe.

The author would like to express heartfelt thanks to Karl Rohe, Johann Friedl, Utz Haltern and Wilhelm Ribhegge, whose basic contributions made completion of the work possible.

Münster/Westphalia
HEINZ GOLLWITZER

3 Dreams of a Russo-Asian empire: binding design of E. Ukhtomsky's
Travels in the East (1895–96 edition)

I THE IMPERIALIST AGE

No epoch can be reduced to a single common denominator. To use the concept 'imperialist age' signifies an attempt to pinpoint and summarize powerful trends of an era; to establish the relationship between widely held views, between political and economic attitudes, and between public, scientific and literary pronouncements. In other words, having shown the presence of a particular 'epoch style' and a supra-national mental affinity, to set out the achievements and effects of imperialist thought and action. This does not indicate, however, that an epoch can be completely encompassed by such means. Quite apart from the possibility that a full insight cannot be obtained until we are at a greater distance from the period concerned, there are numerous events and movements between the 1880s and the First World War which may certainly be included among the prerequisites for imperialism, but must primarily be understood as independent phenomena: for example, the emancipation of the worker, women and youth; technical and industrial progress; new cultural horizons; and the decline in Church authority over men's minds and of Christian belief. Moreover, during the imperialist epoch there were at least as many, if not more, anti-imperialists as convinced imperialists in individual states, not to mention the large masses who were indifferent. And a number of medium- and smaller-sized states, which had no colonial possessions, were not at first confronted with the problems of imperialism, even if they eventually became enmeshed in imperialist politics – during the course of the First World War at the latest.

Although a considerable number of 'empires' (in the sense of the domination of several peoples by one realm) have been known since antiquity, the term 'imperialist age' has been current only since the close of the nineteenth century. The situation which emerged at that time must have been quite unusual to justify the introduction of this new expression. The history of the word 'imperialism' gives, as a rule, insufficient information on the concept and the conditions which gave birth to it. Apart from individual use in other connections, imperialism was first spoken about in France under Louis-Philippe. The word was then used to express the idea that the Citizen King's régime was capable of powerful political action. 'Imperialism' took on the character of a slogan during the time of Napoleon III. People, however, were more interested in the person of the emperor and his political system than in his empire as a connection between France and her territories outside Europe; when using the word 'imperialism' people thought more of modern dictatorship than of the creation of an imperial realm. Anyone speaking of 'imperialism' in relation to Bonapartist France meant the internal order of the Napoleonic state. When the word 'imperialism' found acceptance in Great Britain as a specialized political term in the third quarter of the nineteenth century, the concept had lost practically all its domestic overtones. Yet in fact they persisted very strongly, and it is one of the tasks of this book to prove their continuance. Around 1900 imperialism was understood to be an extension of national policies into active world policies. It had come to mean empire-building on the basis of colonial acquisitions, of increases in navies and armies as instruments of such policies, of a position at the 'top table' among the world powers with consequent acceptance into their ranks and, the nearer the First World War loomed, of an ever-increasing zeal in the creation of European alliances with world-wide scope. For those living at the turn of the century, imperialism signified continued exports and foreign investments on behalf of the home economy with strong protective measures on the part of the home government to maintain them. But it was also taken to indicate their employment for promoting or consolidating a position of world power. The acceptance of imperialism finally meant that its adherents had become attracted, and let themselves be guided, by the idea of a world mission for individual nations, the thoughts behind the so-called 'pan' movements, and many other similar doctrines.

Taking as a basis what was held to be a matter of course in 1900, we can interpret imperialist policy today as the expansionist power policies of the larger European countries, North America and Japan. These policies were usually closely bound up with the interests of various branches of the national economy of the period; occasionally national policy functioned almost as an executive organ of financial power groups. But the very opposite – exploitation of the economy for the purposes of the state – repeatedly occurred; and powerful economic circles, though originally uninterested in imperialism, often adopted the state-dictated course in the conviction that the future belonged to the imperialist style of politics and economics. The achievements in the sphere of nationalist imperialism by leading expansionist politicians, with industrial, trade and banking magnates at their elbows, were counterbalanced by bigtime operators who contrived to build up economic empires on an international scale more or less outside the control of the state. These independent economic empires undoubtedly became involved in many ways in the policies of the world powers, but had nevertheless taken over the principles of conquest and organization for their own use with considerable success, and had overcome the national ties of the majority of their contemporaries without much soul-searching.

Imperialist politics can never be understood from the point of view of economics alone. Imperialism, in the consciousness of the masses and by its very nature, was determined far more by 'autonomous' policies, by the actions of leading statesmen and political spokesmen, who felt responsible for securing the existence of their countries and raising the standards of living. The maintenance and increase of state prestige on a world-wide scale represented a no less important and integral trend in the pluralistic make-up of imperialist policy than the hopes of the economy for a favourable solution of export and import problems, or the attainment of good rates of interest on excess capital. Statesmen of the period did not consider problems of self-assertion or the extension of power by leading countries to be occurrences merely in the realm of economic competition: they were no less intent on achieving these aims by strengthening their armed forces on land and sea, by the acquisition of strategic positions and bases throughout the world, and by gaining territory. These new territorial areas were coveted more often for the chances they afforded of extending power by their very existence or geographical location, than for any economic advantages they offered. Such trains of thought did not willy-nilly have to find expression in a permanent drive for offensive action or aggression, but they at least made continuous political initiative on a global scale necessary.

Turkey was certainly an empire in the sense of the domination by one dynasty and one nation over numerous countries and peoples. But the fact that she was more an object than a subject of international politics prior to the First World War, and that she could only adopt a defensive attitude, by and large precludes the designation of 'imperial' in her case. When the leading circles of the Habsburg monarchy began to fear for the continuance of their state as a great power, they perceived the solution to this difficult situation in a transition from a predominantly defensive and stone-walling policy to one of imperialism. To adopt an imperialist policy meant putting in a bid for world recognition and having a say in all the great events of world politics. When Spain had to give up almost all the remaining components of her imperialist façade at the end of the nineteenth century, the loss plunged the nation into a deep internal crisis. The Spaniard's *amour-propre* was more painfully involved at that time than the Englishman's when Britain was forced to dismantle her colonial empire after 1945 – which also illustrates how desperately the consciousness of political prestige had clutched at imaginary imperial greatness.

Even a provisional sketch of imperialism's main character-istics must contain a reference to its ideological make-up. Events of an imperialist nature can be observed before the time of 'classical' imperialism. It is primarily the appearance of a principle that introduces the 'classic' element, a principle mainly reflected in the new imperialist ideologies. Heinrich Friedjung, coiner of the expression 'the age of imperialism', saw as one of its most important characteristics, 'that the power impulse became conscious, and was thus elevated to a directive for action'. There is, however, no watertight, unified doctrine of imperialism. The ideological spectrum reveals profound differences from nation to nation, and also represents an eclectic entity in its supra-national constituents.

Even a cursory examination of imperialism's intellectual basis as a world movement reveals two opposing tendencies: first, a group of ideologies which exist within the framework of traditional civilization, systems of thought with a humanitar-ian, idealist or Christian cast; and second, ideologies which can be reduced to the common denominator of so-called Social Darwinism. The importance of both trends for their era and the influence they exerted on the thoughts and actions of millions are worthy of particular note. These imperialist ideologies, however, as has already been stressed, were never generally accepted despite their wide currency. Nor should one forget the millions who could not (or not yet) be reached ideologically, and those others who, without being anti-imperialist, persisted stubbornly in maintaining older political views. Imperialist activities and attitudes of mind, despite all their democratic tendencies, have always remained the preserve of minorities. The decisive factor is that the imperialists, to-gether with the socialists, embodied the modern and dynamic element of their time, and should be regarded as the 'moving force' of the age.

The identification or designation of an epoch can be counted as one of the historian's most important tasks. The difficulty lies in the complicated nature of each age, particularly in the overlapping of different phases. An effort of constructive experiment is therefore necessary to characterize an era. It is impossible to reproduce a past epoch adequately; it all depends on recognizing when new characteristic tendencies begin to take over and when they again cease to dominate. Actions of an imperialist nature, as has already been mentioned, have occurred before and after the epoch normally termed 'imperialist'. It is a good thing therefore to distinguish between imperialist policies in general which may crop up at any time and are not tied to any particular era, and a clearly defined imperialist age. It is only with the latter that we are here concerned.

What is it that distinguishes this epoch from the one that preceded it, and from which point of time do the words 'the imperialist age' no longer apply? There has been no lack of attempts to set the beginning of this epoch at an earlier date. We cannot overlook, for example, the fact that decades before the 1880s the Tsarist Empire had fulfilled all the prerequisites of an imperialist, expansionist policy in its struggle with Turkey and Persia, in the 'pacification' of the Caucasus, in the conquest of Central Asia and the rush forward into the Far East. The strong influence exercised by Russia in central and south-eastern Europe must be added to this. The policy of St Petersburg rested on a mighty military organization and, finally, there were tendencies towards a pan-Slav ideology even before the middle of the century. Countering this, Soviet Russian historians have pointed to the early start of imperialist policies carried out by the great powers in the Far East. In order to prove the impact of the imperialism of Free Trade, Western historians have even counted the number of areas annexed by Great Britain in Asia and Africa during the almost unrestricted sway of Free Trade principles. There was never any question of surrendering India even when other colonies were regarded as 'millstones round the neck'. Quite the contrary occurred at that very time when the British government deprived the East India Company of the right to administer the most important territory outside Europe and took the reins into their own hands. 'Thus the mid-Victorian period now appears as an era of large-scale expansion', write Gallagher and Robinson 'and the late-Victorian age does not seem to introduce any significant novelty into that process of expansion.' The fact is that there are no caesuras and no revolutionary events which, so to speak, changed the scene completely and unequivocally overnight in favour of an imperialist epoch.

There exist, nevertheless, certain criteria which enable us to distinguish between imperialist and merely imperial policy, and between an imperialist age and other epochs which preceded or followed it. When a strong tendency appears towards imperial consolidation or expansion, and matters of global politics assume a central place in the government programme, we may speak of an imperialist phase on the part of the state leadership. It can be truly said, for instance, that Tsar Nicholas I used imperial power policies in Europe and Asia; yet the maintenance of the legitimist principle and the traditional social order in Europe took clear priority over all ideas of conquest or plans for expansion. The power politics inherent in certain isolated decisions and actions of Gladstone's governments do not disprove the fact that his cabinets actually concentrated on the internal reform and economic advancement of Great Britain. On the other hand, we may well speak of true imperialism when we consider the Russian state's temporary concentration on an aggressive policy in the Far East under Tsar Nicholas II or Joseph Chamberlain's success at the turn of the century in getting the policy-makers of the day to climb

4 Great Britain and Russia taking a mutual 'footbath' in Asia; an Austrian cartoon of 1894

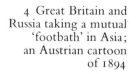

15

on his bandwagon. Certain of Napoleon III's measures and velleities do not entitle us to talk of an imperialist system in the way we use the term today, nor to ascribe to them the character of the epoch we are describing. But the setting up of an Indo-Chinese and African colonial empire by the Third Republic may certainly be called imperialism. The acquisition of German colonies alone did not turn Bismarck into an imperialist states-man. Wilhelm II, on the other hand, may be taken as an exponent of German imperialism; he approved and advocated his country's active participation in world politics, even if his success at expansion turned out to be rather modest. The activity of the state leadership would not be enough to make us call the epoch 'imperialist', especially as it cannot be said at all that the cabinets were totally committed to imperialist pro-grammes and convictions even during the 'age of imperialism' itself. It was indispensable that the consciousness of leading groups identify itself with the imperialist programme, that the new convictions gain a foothold in public opinion, and that imperialism spread not only as a practice but also as an intel-lectual movement. Finally, the imperialist epoch reveals changes in internal politics and in the ensemble of social forces. All this taken together was what gave the imperialist age its character-istic stamp: the fact that imperialist modes of thought forced their way into cabinets and parliaments, and could be raised by ideologists to a general maxim of politics; the appearance of imperialist organizations and pressure groups; the founding of imperialist institutions; and finally the increasing intensity of reflection on power politics. The style of the epoch was evolved by the interplay of all these factors. Close cooperation by governments, business circles and centres of propaganda brought about more rational and systematic empire-building. Great Britain was in the vanguard, but other great powers both in and outside Europe – some at the time and some even before her – trod the path of imperialist expansion.

If we look back to the beginning of the epoch we are forced to ask ourselves what caused the collective and psychological

5 The defeat of France in the 1870–71 war was one of the signal events of the second half of the nineteenth century, and led to a realignment of European power. This painting by Anton von Werner shows the architect of victory, Bismarck, in the very hall where the Versailles Treaty was signed almost fifty years later

changes which made the imperialist age possible. It seems to be rather difficult to answer the question of whether alternatives could have been found. Or, to raise another question: is there enough empirical evidence to explain fully why the leading minorities changed their mentality? Finally, it should be noted that the driving force towards imperialism arose from varying national aspects. In Britain, for example, it sprang from the opposition to doctrinaire Manchesterism and the Little Englanders, while in France it was due to the efforts for the 're-habilitation de la France vaincue' as compensation for her reduced European influence following the lost war of 1870–71. As far as the general supra-national features of imperialism are concerned, it may be assumed that certain events and experiences made the groups in question ripe for acceptance of the imperialist idea. Among these experiences may be counted the fact that an age of global politics had finally arrived following many previous moves in that direction, such as the emancipation of North and South America with its world-wide effects, or the emergence of the 'Oriental question'. This age of world politics existed in the sense of an indissoluble global connection between all important political phenomena and events. The awareness of the growing international interdependence of politics had reached its first climax. Overseas competition by other powers seemed a greater challenge than ever before; ways and means to counter it had to be devised. In addition, the emergence of the German Reich in 1871 made a strong and lasting impression which increased, in its turn, the widespread estimation of the power and majesty of the state. The creation of the 'Bismarck Reich' ended the process of forming powerful European national states. The projection of the 'national state' mentality into world politics led to imperial strivings based on European rivalries, which, although encompassing the globe, still remained narrowly national at the core. Finally, mention should be made of what was certainly not the least of the mass stirrings of the time: the great social conflicts, the class war, which imperialism tried in its own way to counter.

II THE DEMOGRAPHIC SITUATION AND THE TECHNICAL REVOLUTION IN NATURAL SCIENCE

Before examining the historical events and significance of imperialism, it is necessary to establish details of the background against which the events of the age took place. Of primary interest is the increase in population in the nineteenth and twentieth centuries – one of the most important factors in history. The following population changes have been given for the European nations between 1800 and 1914:

Population (in millions)

	Great Britain	Russia	France	Germany	Italy
1796		29			
1800	10·9			24·5	18·1
1801			27·3		
1830	16·5			29·6	
1831			31·9		
1850	20·9			35·4	23
1851			35·8		
1858		67			
1870	26·2			40·9	26·6
1871			36·1		
1897		129			
1900	37			56·4	32·4
1901			39		
1910	40·8				
1911			39·2		34·8
1914		142		67·8	
1921	42		39·2		38·4

These increases in population give the following picture when expressed in density per square kilometre:

Density of Population per square kilometre

	Great Britain	Russia	France	Germany	Italy
1815				46	
1830				55	
1850				66	
1851	91·2		66·5		
1861					85·5
1870				76	
1871	112·4				91·6
1872			67·3		
1881					97·2
1890				91	
1891	140·4		71·5		
..1897		5·8			
1901	156·7		72·6		110·8
1910				120	
1911	172·5		73·8		118·5

This huge growth primarily affected the towns. Urbanization is a phenomenon which changed not only the landscape of Europe but also the organization of society and ways of life. The following list of population increases in European cities speaks for itself:

Population of Cities (Number of inhabitants in thousands)[1]

	London[2]	Paris	Berlin	Vienna	St Petersburg	Rome
1800	831	547	173[3]	247	220	153
1850	2362	1053	420	444	485	175
1880	3779	2269	1122	726	877	300
1900	4536	2714	1899	1675	1133	463[4]
1910	4521	2888	2071	2030	1907	590

[1] Details in round figures.
[2] Details for London (county) for the years 1801, 1851, 1881, 1901, 1911. The rise in population for the Greater London' area grew from 1,114 in 1801 to 7,251 in 1911.
[3] Figure for 1801.
[4] Figure for 1901.

It was not only the metropolises, the main centres of industry, trade, administration and the military, that were affected by this increase, but indeed every city. Another result of the population explosion was that European countries, without running the risk of becoming depopulated themselves, were able to provide millions of emigrants for abroad:

6, 7 One of the results of the great population increase that took place ▶ in most European countries in the late nineteenth century was the growth of large crowded cities. Above, London c. 1896; below, Berlin at the turn of the century

Emigration– Exodus from British Ports (in thousands)

	Total Number	To the USA	To British North America	To Australia and New Zealand	Other Countries
1831–40	703	308	322	68	5
1841–50	1649	1095	429	127	34
1861–70	1572	1133	130	267	42
1881–90	2559	1714	302	378	170
1891–1900	1743	1146	187	128	282

Russia – Registered Emigration Surplus (in thousands)

1876–80 18; 1886–90 124; 1895–1900 158; 1906–10 370; 1911–14 439

German Emigration (in thousands)

1830–38 210; 1850–59 1161

	Total	USA	Canada	Brazil	Remaining Latin American Countries	Australia	Other Countries
1871–75	394	361	1	12	2	5	14
1891–95	402	372	11	8	6	2	4
1901–05	146	135	1	3	2	1	5
1911–13	69	52	1	1	13	1	1

Emigration from France was insignificant, as only the colonies (North Africa) and the USA were the destinations of large groups of emigrants. About 400,000 people emigrated from France to the French colonies from 1861 to 1910 and 260,000 to the USA in the same period of time.

Thus during the nineteenth and twentieth centuries emigrations and population shifts occurred which quantitatively put everything that had previously taken place in the shade. Outstanding historical results of this process are the part emigration played in strengthening the United States, and the ability of several British overseas possessions to raise themselves to the status of independent commonwealths.

Several European countries now show a certain stagnation in the population figures, following the sharp rise in the demographic curve during the nineteenth century. This stagnation dates from the turn of the century and remained unnoticed for some time only because of the general increase in life expectancy. The development began in France and became more and more obvious in Britain from about 1890, in Switzerland from 1905 and in Germany from 1910. Apart from the increased use of birth-control methods, the settling down of the European population to a fairly constant level may be traced back to the attainment of a certain standard of living in an industrial society. Europeans were so devoted to protecting this standard that the majority were even prepared to restrict procreation. It should not be overlooked, however, that those countries in Europe which were not industrialized or only slightly industrialized have remained outside the course of this population curve; and this is especially true of populations outside Europe. Europe's share in the total world population increased during the nineteenth century from an estimated fifth to a fourth, but a retrogressive process set in during the twentieth century. The increase in the number of Asians and Africans was overwhelming, and not only Europe but the whole white population fell numerically behind. As the results of statistical investigations were no secret to the civilized populations, there was no lack of gloomy prophecies during the age of imperialism and later about the future fate of the white man. Original Malthusian ideas may be discovered frequently enough in imperialist thinking, but there is a predominance of what might be called 'prophetic Malthusianism' as the prediction of future dangers. The point to be noted, as far as the period in question is concerned, is that European expansion in its imperialist phase was undoubtedly bound up with the presence of large population reserves in the principal participating nations.

Though the European 'population explosion' of the nineteenth century, as well as the later settling down in the highly industrialized countries, are closely connected with scientific development, the latter's effects on the imperialist age are by no means confined to the demographic sector. Indeed, they are so comprehensive that the term 'scientific revolution' or 'second industrial revolution' is used with justification for the last third of the nineteenth century. G. Barraclough writes:

> The second industrial revolution was different. For one
> thing, it was far more deeply scientific, far less dependent on
> the 'inventions' of 'practical' men with little if any basic
> scientific training. It was concerned not so much to improve
> and increase the existing as to introduce new commodities.
> It was also far quicker in its impact, far more prodigious in
> its results, far more revolutionary in its effects on people's
> lives and outlook. And finally, though coal and iron were
> still the foundation, it could no longer be called the revolu-
> tion of coal and iron. The age of coal and iron was succeeded,
> after 1870, by the age of steel and electricity, of oil and
> chemicals.

There are different groups of scientific discoveries, and inventions
connected with them, in the framework of the second industrial
revolution. They quickly became intertwined, giving each
other mutual support and promotion. As the application of the
steam-engine principle to various other types of machines
initially made possible the great upswing in commercial life
during the first industrial revolution, so the combination of
several scientific discoveries and technical inventions since the
end of the nineteenth century, and their various applications
to production, have had revolutionary effects. They can be
broken down as follows:

Electrotechnics
Development of low-voltage current techniques for trans-
mitting signals (the Reis telephone in 1861 improved by Bell
and Gray in 1876); the tremendous advance in wireless telegraphy based on discoveries by Hertz and Marconi; the invention of the dynamo by Werner Siemens in 1867, which led
to the rise in high-voltage current techniques; the production
of the first electric locomotive by Siemens in 1879; Edison's
invention of the incandescent bulb in the same year; the
erection of the first electric power plant in New York in 1882;

24

8 A tribute to the triumph of steam and electricity on the occasion of ▶
Queen Victoria's Diamond Jubilee in 1897

and the first hydroelectric generating station in Colorado in 1890.

Chemistry

The development of synthetic dyestuffs in Germany; the discovery of dynamite by Nobel in 1867 together with important discoveries in the field of ammunition and explosives; extraction of soda by Ludwig Mond in 1873; production of the first metal carbides through introduction of electrothermal methods by Moissan in 1892; discovery of nickel-carbonyl by Mond in 1890, used as an intermediary product in the manufacture of pure nickel; manufacture of ammonia in England by the Mond gas process, in Germany by the Haber-Bosch process; air-liquefying by Linde in 1895; discovery of radium by the Curies in 1898.

Transport

Invention of the combustion engine in 1877 (four-stroke cycle engine: Otto); high-speed gasoline engine Daimler-Maybach; Benz automobile (1885); manufacture of the pneumatic tyre by Dunlop in 1890; development of the Diesel motor in 1893–7; first flight of a dirigible in 1900; first flight with engine-driven aircraft (Wright brothers) in 1903.

Biology

Discovery of the rules governing heredity (Mendel) in 1865–9; doctrine of mutation (de Vries) in 1901.

The application of electrolysis to chemical processes, the electrochemical field as a whole, or the combination of electricity with the combustion engine, are only a few examples of how the great advances in technical progress merged into a system which changed the face of the globe. Among the most important industrial results of this system may be counted the increase in steel production brought about by the processing methods introduced by Henry Bessemer in 1856, and improved by the inventions of Siemens, the Martin brothers in 1856–64 and of S. G. Thomas and P. C. Gilchrist in 1877.

The expansion of the chemical industry was no less important. Lord Melchett, son of the inventor and entrepreneur, Ludwig Mond, based the British chemical trust known as Imperial Chemical Industries Ltd on his father's firm with even greater organizational success. He also merged the Mond Nickel Co. with the American nickel group in 1928, forming the world trust of International Nickel Co., Canada. Several German firms of large production capacity joined together to form the 'I. G. Farben' trust in 1925, having already gone through various stages of amalgamation beforehand. Low- and high-tension electrical techniques were developed in the electro-technical industry, which made possible, among other things, a new dimension in news dissemination and contributed to the modernization of numerous commercial undertakings by introducing the electric motor. The founding of the AEG in Berlin in 1883 was an outstanding event in the history of this branch of industry. In the field of transport, the ground was laid for those world operations whose main development did not take place until after the First World War. And the petroleum industry rose to importance correspondingly.

When the chemical discoveries or Mendel's laws and their practical application became common property, the prerequisites were created for more rational plant cultivation and animal breeding, and thus for a considerable increase in agricultural production. Enormous changes were brought about by natural science and technical inventions in the field of medicine. Antisepsis and asepsis, bacteriology, general anaesthetics, the use of X-rays, research into vitamins and hormones, new methods of combating contagious diseases and, last but not least, advances in pharmaceuticals, extended considerably the frontiers of medical science and practice.

Daily life was revolutionized by these achievements of science, technology and industry. Transport gradually left the era of the 'iron horse' and entered that of the motor car and

Deuxième Salon du Cycle

PALAIS DE L'INDUSTRIE

9, 10 Advances in the field of transportation were an important aspect of the technological revolution. Above, the ubiquitous bicycle; opposite, an early glorification of the automobile

aeroplane; the electric tramcar and the taxi succeeded the horse-drawn omnibus and carriage on city streets. These changes, it is true, took place at a leisurely pace, and compared with today's conditions they may be regarded as only a preparatory stage. All the masses could afford at first was a bicycle or trips by rail or tram. It may be added that the history of transport is not different from any other branch of history: no one epoch disappears abruptly to make way for the next. But the basis for the new transport situation, which has since become an economic and political factor of prime importance, was already laid in the age of imperialism. The new means of communication emanating from the scientific or second industrial revolution had already reached a noteworthy degree of perfection before the First World War: the telephone and telegraph did their part in increasing the tempo and circulation of the period and promoting the inner coalescence of the world. Contributions by the cinematograph and gramophone were meagre at first, but the achievements which came later were already recognized in principle. Chemistry helped the production of synthetics, which began in textiles, building and other branches of industry. The essence of nutrition was changed

11 French caricature of the air traffic of the future (1901)

by refrigeration techniques and canning. Only now did it become possible to transport large quantities of various foodstuffs to Europe from distant countries. Mass production by the new food industries catered for the mass population. The invention of the machine-gun in 1883, the introduction of heavy weapons and armoured battleships, the first designs for submarines and tanks – all ushered in a new era. Finally, the invention of the typewriter in 1867 had its social effects on history. The figure of the scribe, familiar for thousands of years, departed from the scene and the shorthand-typist took his place.

Today we are obviously in the middle of a third industrial revolution, more indebted to science for support and guidance than either of its two predecessors. Some of the discoveries which led to this – especially those in the realm of atomic physics – had already been made between 1880 and 1918, and it can be said in general that our present social level rests on foundations laid in the last third of the nineteenth century.

It should be emphasized that not only the economic and social structures had to adapt themselves to the upheavals of the age, but also the state itself. This does not mean that the state, the economy and society at large were a prey to unnamed and indiscriminate forces emanating from the demographic sphere or to the emergence of a supposedly omnipotent technical-scientific civilization. The state and the economy themselves developed strong initiatives and both provided a relatively stable edifice for numerous movements and innovations, and also supplied an adequate concept of order.

III THE WORLD POLITICAL CONSTELLATION

The great political decisions between 1880 and 1918 were made, no longer exclusively, but mainly in Europe. Their scope, however, gave them an increasing aura of world politics. Events in Europe and other parts of the world began to interact more intensively. Nor did the rest of the world remain merely an area of confrontation for the great powers of Europe; the United States and Japan not only assumed the role of great powers, but became world powers which intervened in international politics.

The creation of the German national state, which coincided with the formation of the Italian national state, was the foremost event on the eve of the imperialist age. Seen through the eyes of the German and Italian peoples, this meant the fulfilment of an urgent longing for unity harboured by the most active and intelligent strata of the nation, and possibly of catching up with the Western countries who had already been luckier in this respect. The ambivalence of the event, viewed equally in terms of foreign and domestic policies, becomes clear when it is realized that both nations thus became politically independent and capable of competing with their neighbours. The events of 1870–71 shifted the centres of gravity in European politics. Berlin, in particular, grew from the role of a capital in a state already considered a great power into a gravitation centre of the first rank. The weight of the new German position was increased by the political genius of Prince Bismarck, the Reichschancellor, who understood how to keep the reins of European politics in his hands for the twenty years before his eclipse, even if this meant adopting methods of a continually more complicated nature. During his period of office, 1871–90, no international agreement of any significance was arrived at without his participation or against his will.

It may be doubted whether Bismarck would have been fortunate enough to preserve this incomparable position had his period of office lasted longer, and it is still more unlikely that his successors would have been able to maintain the continental preponderance of Bismarckian Germany for many years to come. What caused this preponderance? Primarily the fact that Bismarck succeeded in isolating his vanquished opponent, France, and prevented her from finding powerful allies that might have assisted in reversing the events of 1871. When Bismarck favoured the colonial policies of the Third Republic, it was obvious that his purpose was to divert France towards new aims which could not harm Germany. The Reichs-chancellor tried to secure the fruits of the Franco-German War by working for cooperation between the Hohenzollern, the Habsburg and the Tsarist empires, the 'League of the Three Emperors', which had the additional purpose of defending the monarchical principle and authoritarianism. In many respects this recalled the Holy Alliance. But the conservatism of that period was unable to support any further blocs and – this proved more decisive – Russia's foreign policy aims tended to collide more and more with those of Germany and Austria-

12 German cartoon of Bismarck ('unified Germany') with Europe under his control (1875)

32

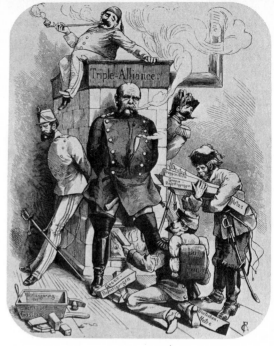

13 The Triple Alliance between Germany, Austria and Italy was established in 1882. This German cartoon of 1883 asserts that the Alliance was impervious to French and Russian attempts to upset it, and also shows Bismarck's dominating position in European affairs at that time

Hungary. Despite their extremely different systems of internal politics, the rapprochement between Russia and the Third Republic had been noticeable ever since the first five years following the Treaty of Frankfurt in 1871. Bismarck succeeded, however, in preventing Germany's links with St Petersburg from being shattered despite several grave crises, and was even able to cooperate in maintaining the Austro-Russian connections until 1887. He warded off the immediate threat to German-Russian relations during the final phase of his power by means of the so-called 'Reinsurance Treaty'. But the only ally in the real sense of the word left to the Hohenzollern Empire from the Triple Alliance was the Habsburg monarchy. In favour of Berlin, the latter suspended its foreign policy activities to a considerable extent in Paris and London, and concentrated more on south-eastern Europe instead. The dual alliance which had existed between Germany and Austria since 1879 was joined by Italy in 1882 and Rumania in 1883. The Mediterranean Treaty of 1887 between Austria, Great Britain and Italy, directed against France and Russia, must also be counted as a success for Bismarck's policies. The continental system of

33

pacts remained unopposed by any kind of anti-German alliance until Bismarck fell from power.

Although Bismarck's system of alliances achieved great successes, it must be remembered that continental politics were overshadowed by a sphere of world politics in which Bismarck's Germany played almost no part and in which Britain and Russia were the main protagonists. From the 1880s it was evident that France was becoming the third European partner in this sphere. The 'new course' which Germany followed after Bismarck's dismissal in 1890 also meant that the compass was set in the direction of world politics. Italy's attempts to participate in the imperialist game turned out to be less convincing. It was of far greater universal historical significance that the United States and Japan, by the turn of the century, had secured their places as partners in the world system of imperialist politics. The policies centred on Europe were not superseded by a global political system within this period; but the interweaving of European and extra-European politics on a world-wide scale was from the very beginning the hall-mark of the imperialist age. In this connection the front line between the British and Russian spheres of expansion, which ran right through Asia from the Turkish straits to India, seemed to contemporaries at the end of the nineteenth century to be an axis of presumably lasting and perhaps unchangeable antagonism. This chain of conflict zones, consisting of the Ottoman Empire, Persia and Afghanistan, assumed actual world political significance, but it was very soon to appear that one could speak only in a limited sense of an inevitable conflict between Britain and Russia over their Asian interests. At any rate both proved capable of overcoming the crises which occurred at regular intervals, without recourse to arms. A partial settlement was always reached, even if it was no complete solution, and the continuing rivalry was ultimately subordinated to common political interests in Europe. The establishment of a French colonial empire in Indo-China and in large tracts of Africa constituted a further event of far-reaching consequences in world politics. Before the end of the century this development led to considerable friction with Great Britain. The prime example of this was the Fashoda crisis, which was symptomatic of the unclear and contrary aims of both nations in Egypt and the Sudan. This constellation was also to be altered in the first decade of the twentieth century.

The Spanish-American War of 1898 signalled the entry of the United States into imperialist world politics, and despite several retarding factors and frequent strong counterblasts in North America, the clock could not be turned back. This would have happened in any case in view of the enormous power of the United States in the one world then forming. The transitory entry of the United States into the ranks of the colonial powers had relatively minor effects. Its presence on the world political scene and the opportunity to have its say in all the great matters of world politics (which it frequently used)

14 The British presence in Egypt: troops at the Pyramids after the bombardment of Alexandria in 1882

L'ÉPÉE DE DAMOCLES

15 'The sword of Damocles': French cartoon (1903) on the threat of Japan to Russia

applied mainly to Latin America, China and, not least, to the disputes just then beginning with Japan. The 'open door' principle upheld by the United States overseas, which was actually a non-imperialist concept, had to be put into practice within the framework of a general imperialist world and power policy, and therefore had to undergo considerable modification.

Japan, the great power in the Far East, had been recognized as such since her successful war against China in 1894–95. Her position was strengthened by the alliance with Great Britain in 1902, and her victory over Russia in 1904–05 finally opened the door to world power. Japan gave the world the first example of a completely emancipated Asiatic state.

The large and valuable overseas possessions of the Netherlands and Portugal can only be termed peripheral phenomena in the political power-play of the world at that time. Likewise the modest successes attained by Germany and Italy in attempting to acquire territories outside Europe remained episodes of little importance against the general background of historical development. Mere possession of colonies was still insufficient for acceptance of partnership in imperialist competition. Germany proved that the establishment of an efficient industry, world-wide trade, capital exports, technical achievements in foreign countries and demonstrations of military strength could lead to an expansionist policy despite widely dispersed and therefore weak overseas positions. It certainly proved at the same time how the number of international friction points could be increased.

The extension of her area of activity, which was as inevitable as the entry of other nations into the capitalist and imperialist epoch, did not allow Germany to keep the pre-eminent European position she had assumed in the time of Bismarck. France succeeded in liberating herself from isolation, and the conclusion of the Franco-Russian alliance of 1894 showed that another system now confronted the Triple Alliance. The

16 Russian postcard (*c*. 1902) on the attitudes of Britain and the United States in the Russo-Japanese conflict

Généraux avec la jumelle Franco-Rousse   Colonels avec le sabre Franco-Rousse   Lieutenants avec l'epée Franco-Rousse   Tambours-majors avec la canne Franco

Anglo-French agreement of 1904 on mutual interests in Egypt and Morocco laid the foundation for the *entente* of western Europe's dominant powers. When, contrary to general expectations, agreements were reached between Russia and Britain on the demarcation of spheres of interest in Persia, Afghanistan and Tibet, the power combination began to take shape which was to measure up to and conquer the so-called Central Powers in the First World War.

Great Britain's ties with France and Russia did not take on the character of an alliance until 1914. From the standpoint of diplomacy and international law, she maintained a free hand until the very last, that is to say, until deciding to intervene in the First World War. But in the general trend of foreign policy, she definitely and increasingly veered more towards France and Russia than towards the German Empire, which insisted on building up its fleet and in this way (although not in this way alone) manœuvred itself into a position of strong opposition *vis-à-vis* Britain. And, as the First World War showed, one cannot overestimate the friendship between Britain and the United States as being one of the most powerful and effective constellations of world politics during the age of imperialism.

Agreements and conversations between the leading statesmen, talks among the general staffs, military and naval conventions, manipulation of financial capital for political aims, mutual visits by heads of state, and particularly the cultivation of public opinion by the press on both sides, made a decisive

Clairon Franco-Russe   Tambour Franco-Russe   Contre-basse Franco-Russe   Grosse-caisse Franco-Russe

17 Contemporary caricature of the Franco-Russian military alliance of 1894

contribution towards consolidating and stiffening the political and military systems. Actually there was no dearth of constructive compromises in cases of opposing international interests during the age of imperialism. In addition to the Anglo-French-Russian agreements, there were also (among others) the solution of the Samoa crisis through Bismarck's compliance; the clearing up of German-Spanish colonial disputes; German-French and Anglo-German agreements on Morocco, the Cameroons and the construction of the Baghdad Railway; Anglo-German agreements on the future treatment of the Portuguese colonial possessions. This tendency towards peaceful compromise, however, was confronted by a more powerful policy of force and subjection, preventative rather than aggressive, which, if not exactly warlike, still depended on pressure and dangerous methods. The risk that tensions between the two power blocs might lead to war was great. But who wishes to assert that this event was absolutely unavoidable and would have to take place in the manner that it actually did? According to present research, the First World War, in which the age of imperialism experienced its catastrophic climax at the same time that the contours of a new epoch became visible, was unleashed more by fear than arbitrary action or as a result of many years' planning. It is important to know the mentality and motives of those leading statesmen who had to bear the responsibility for the outbreak of the war, and the diplomatic history immediately preceding it. But for our purpose it is more interesting to explain the war, its character and premises within the pattern of the age. Considered from this angle we understand the First World War as the result of imperialist antagonism generated by pact systems competing on a world scale, policies of prestige and compensation, the armaments race, the lack of an effective supra-national authority, institutionalized jealousy and mistrust in principle of the procedural methods for conducting international relations, which were primitive though technically highly developed. It would have to be the subject of a special and difficult investigation to find out to what extent social and inner political tensions in the substratum of events accelerated the readiness to engage in war on a large scale, quite apart from the imperialist rivalry of the great empires and national hatred between peoples. The outbreak of the First World War, however, can be attributed to neither social nor ideological disputes, although these came increasingly to the fore during the war years and had a considerable share in the political decisions at its end. The attitude of organized labour, for example, was an important consideration for the leading statesmen even at the start of hostilities.

18 The international dispute over Morocco: a French cartoon of 190.

IV NATIONALISM; 'PAN' MOVEMENTS; EMPIRE IDEOLOGIES

HER MOST GRACIOUS MAJESTY.

Our Queen and our Empress
Is greater and wiser
Than all foreign monarchs,
Including "der Kaiser."

19 British nationalism: illustration and jingle from a book for children (1876)

Lord Rosebery recognized that nationalism was the seed of imperialism when he spoke of 'that greater pride in Empire which is called Imperialism and is a larger patriotism'. It was the consolidated national state which provided the primary base in the nineteenth and twentieth centuries from which a nation could reach out towards the rest of the world. The psychic disposition to a *ne plus ultra* attitude was reached only when pride in former political and cultural achievements, in the excellence of the national character and the inherent genius of the nation itself, had developed to a high degree; when national self-confidence dominated all public pronouncements, and national traditions were raised to the level of cultural standards. People began to cherish the idea of having a mission to fulfil, they tried to solve world problems and lend the mantle of considered thought to the phenomena of political and economic expansion which had hitherto had an overwhelmingly pragmatic character. They sought to endow the latter with a

41

more elevated meaning – in a word, to turn them into an ideology. The transition from nationalism to imperialism was evoked in a still higher degree by the increasing intensity of political interrelationship throughout the globe, which spurred the nations on to fiercer international rivalry than ever before and made them seek precautions on a world-wide scale to ward off the seeming danger of national extinction.

In political practice, and especially in the nations' collective consciousness, nationalism and imperialism continued to fuse into one concept; the vast majority of people scarcely made a sharp distinction between the two. Also, during the whole of the imperialist age, nationalism meant more to the masses – at least, in the countries of continental Europe – than 'pan' movements and empire-building. Despite the use of democratic techniques, the introduction of larger organizations and the employment of mass propaganda, the realization of imperialism remained the concern of an intellectual, political and economic *élite*. The same applied in its time to national integration, the predecessor of imperialism. The views held by the broad masses generally lag a generation behind those of the *avant-garde*. When the bolder and more adventurous spirits proceeded to adopt imperialist modes of thought and action in the nineteenth and twentieth centuries, the bulk of the population had just reached the threshold of nationalism. The pacifist-international circles – those whose views were neither nationalist nor imperialist – may be left out of consideration for the time being; nowhere did they constitute a majority.

Imperialist thinking transcended traditional national consciousness in two directions. Firstly, people raised themselves above the limited sphere of their own nations through ethnic and linguistic-cultural groupings; they attained a new dimension by way of pan-Slavism, through Anglo-Saxon, Germanic or Teutonic affiliations, through Latinism or other similar identifications. Secondly, there was the process of empire-building, which embraced different peoples, races and cultures, conferring on the mother country the new role of

20 Vignette from a pan-Slav journal published in Vienna (1865)

'leader state' within an international agglomeration of power, and giving the nation concerned the tasks and position of a leading if not indeed a master race.

Even the autocratic Russia of the nineteenth and early twentieth centuries was forced to influence public opinion and attempt to bring about that harmony of state and society known since the eighteenth century as patriotism and which, having assumed increasingly democratic forms since the French Revolution, became nationalism. We must make a distinction in Russia, as elsewhere, between a patriotism and nationalism inspired and guided from above, on the one hand, and a reformative national movement supported mainly by the intelligentsia, on the other. Both these tendencies, the Slavophile school and the national consciousness fostered from above, remained enemies for a long time. Russian absolutism recognized the democratic character of the Slavophile movement. Numerous leading personalities of non-Russian origin in the Empire were certainly prepared to identify themselves with the idea of the Russian state but not with Russian nationality. Both trends of thought came nearer to each other in a specific way during the second half of the nineteenth century. The religious and conservative traits, which were at least as strong in Slavophile thinking as the reformative ones, made an approach easier. The key word which reflects this development is *narodnost* – a translation of the German word *Volkstum*. It is true that in the 1850s Tsarist ministers and Slavophiles used the word in a different meaning, but finally it was to become a binding formula for national strivings from above and below because of its inherent religious and traditional elements. If one emphasized the ethnic principle as one did by using the concept of *narodnost* it was natural to pay attention to the other Slav peoples, especially as a pan-Slav initiative had already emanated from their ranks. Generally speaking, however, it remained for Russian authors to give a political turn to what were originally the philological and cultural impulses of non-Russian Slavs. After Pushkin's innocuous songs about western Slavs, there appeared the 'Ode to the Slavs' by A. S. Chomyakov in 1832, which spoke of the Russian eagle spreading its protective wings over the Slavs of Germany, Austria and Turkey. Following the March Revolution of 1848, the poet F. J. Tyuchev had visions of a universal monarchy under Russian leadership, based on Slav unity. In 1838 the historian M. P. Pogodin tried to deliver a letter on Russian history to the heir to the throne which must be considered the first programme of political pan-Slavism:

> A people of sixty million, excluding those not recorded, a population which grows by a further million annually and will soon amount to a hundred million! . . . And to this number we may add the thirty million of our brothers and cousins, those Slavs who are scattered across the face of Europe from Constantinople to Venice, from the Morea to the Baltic and North Seas, those Slavs . . . who are bound to us in spiritual unity by origin and language despite geographical and political separation. We can subtract their number from the populations of neighbouring Austria and Turkey and from the rest of Europe. What will then be left to them and what will belong to us?

Chomyakov's 'Ode' was forbidden by Tsar Nicholas's government, Tyuchev could contemplate publication of his political

21 Austrian cartoon on the pan-Slav congress in Moscow in 1867. Czech representatives are approaching for their share of 'pan-Slav milk'

poems only at a much later date, and Pogodin's letter was not printed until 1867. Official St Petersburg was not only afraid of brushes with those European powers whose populations were partially Slav in origin, but was also suspicious of the revolutionary wing of the pan-Slav movement, whose leading exponent was the anarchist Bakunin. According to the standards of the Tsarist régime, a meeting like the first Slav Congress at Prague in 1848 could only be interpreted as high treason. Meanwhile, the overwhelming majority of Russian pan-Slavists were loyal citizens, and the liberal era which followed the succession of Alexander II not only permitted unhindered propaganda but also cross-connections between the highest government officials and prominent leaders of the pan-Slav agitation. Participants in the Moscow Slav Congress of 1867 were already received by the Tsar. In 1871 appeared N. Y. Danilevsky's book, *Russia and Europe*, the standard work on pan-Slavism, which defined Russia's national character as clearly separated from the West and outlined the historical mission of the Slav peoples.

A closer look at the pan-Slav programme shows that it was not thoroughly worked out from a political point of view, let alone from the standpoints of constitutional, public or international law. On the whole it amounted to pan-Russianism rather than pan-Slavism. Non-Russian peoples of Slav origin were not likely, however, to be won over to Russian lordship by the direct approach. For example, the *Address to the Serbs from Moscow*, published by Chomyakov in 1860, caused pronounced annoyance to those addressed because of its dictatorial tone. Besides, in competition with Russian pan-Slavism, there was a movement in Austria for Slav independence and unity – the so-called Austro-Slav movement – which hoped to achieve its aims within the Habsburg Empire. During the 1880s and 1890s pan-Slavism temporarily receded in Russia itself as a political vogue. The government in St Petersburg had never officially given its blessing to the pan-Slav programme, although sometimes making concessions to pan-Slavism or cashing in on its propaganda. The government contented itself with Russification of the non-Slav nationalities inside its state borders.

In the first decade of the twentieth century a new type of 'ennobled' and 'more enlightened' pan-Slavism or 'Neo-Slavism' began to spread. Its Russian spokesmen were more tactful than their predecessors and aimed at a kind of Slav commonwealth. It is remarkable that the initial impetus to this

22 Title-page of Danilevsky's pan-Slav book, *Russia and Europe* (1888 edition), with a portrait of the author

23 The Tsarevich at the Pyramids, 1890–91; photograph from a book by Esper Ukhtomsky, a supporter of Russian imperialism (*see* Ill. 3)

renaissance came again from outside – from Prague and Belgrade – and that for the first time, the support of a powerful Polish movement, Roman Dmovsky's National Democratic Party, was to be reckoned with.

'The Oriental question' was one of the catch phrases frequently heard in the political world of the nineteenth and the beginning of the twentieth centuries. Russian propaganda emphasized the task of the Tsarist Empire, in connection with the Oriental question, to protect or even liberate the Christian Slav minorities under the domination of the Porte. That this problem could only be solved by the roundabout method of striking down the Austro-Hungarian and perhaps the German states – both also considered oppressors of the Slavs – was one of the theses of an aggressive pan-Slavism as expressed, for example, in the pamphlet, *Opinion on the Eastern Question*, published by General Fadeyev in 1871. In the Russian view, the Oriental question meant much more than the mere liberation of the

Slavs in the Balkans; it especially meant the annexation of Constantinople. With this aim in view, the theorists no longer restricted themselves to the 'pan' movement; instead they developed a strong desire to build up the 'World Empire of the Tsars' by acquiring a city of incomparable significance from the point of view of geopolitics and universal history. It had been an aim of Russian policy, long before the age of imperialism, to replace the Crescent by the Cross on Hagia Sophia. This aim was maintained until the collapse of the Tsarist Empire and constituted an essential and inalienable part of the imperialist programme. Dostoyevsky spoke for many others in the following words:

> Russia will never stop serving the Slavs and will always sustain them through her great central strength . . . and should Russia now take in Constantinople, this would happen only because, aside from the solution of the Slav problem, a much greater problem – the Oriental question – is included among her tasks. This can only be solved by the conquest of Constantinople, . . . and the path to salvation is for Russia alone and on her own account to take Constantinople, for only Russia can say confidently that she is equal to the task. And is this not the plain truth? Russia is the spiritual centre, the brain of the east, but the city of Constantinople is the heart of the eastern world.

St Petersburg's empire-building, however, extended in yet another direction. The Russians were more successful in Central Asia, Persia and the Far East, where they succeeded in bringing huge areas into their sphere of influence, partly by conquest and partly by political pressure, than they were in Turkey. Pan-Slavists and 'Easterners' (*Vostokniki*) sometimes confronted one another as rivals in the fields of political action and ideology. But there were also occasions when they both promoted the same aims of Slav fraternization and an Asiatic 'mission' within the plan for a world empire. Dostoyevsky can be quoted again as the mouthpiece of pan-Slavism:

24 The harbour of Vladivostok, capital of Russia's Far East empire

Why is it necessary for us to annex Asia? . . . It is necessary because Russia is not merely a part of Europe but also of Asia, because the Russian is not merely a European but also an Asian. Because our hopes, perhaps, are centred more in Asia than in Europe. Nor is that all: Asia will prove the outlet for our future destiny.

The conquest of the khanates in Central Asia, the provinces of Amur and Ussuri, and the building of Vladivostok ('Mistress of the East') seemed to many politicians and publicists to be the starting-point for still greater things. The anchoring of Russian influence in Manchuria led to dreams of hegemony over all of China. And while individual Russian thinkers, like Vladimir Soloviev, saw their motherland's tasks as the protection of themselves and the rest of Europe from 'the yellow peril' of millions of Chinese possibly under Japanese leadership, Count Esper Ukhtomsky, president of the Russian-Chinese Bank, preached 'Asianism' – the fusion of Russia with the greater Asiatic empires into a peaceful community of peoples under the Tsar. The setback to Russian policy in the Far East after the 49 war with Japan in 1904-05 did not make the Russian imperialists give up all their Far East plans, but it caused them to turn even more to the Slav 'Irredenta' in Austria, to the Balkans and to Constantinople.

The beginnings of imperialism in Great Britain were also bound up with an ideological slant which exceeded mere insular patriotism and put the solidarity and unity of the Anglo-Saxon race throughout the world on a higher plane than the power of the United Kingdom as a state. The brilliant Charles Dilke made himself the spokesman of this outlook. In 1868 he published an account of a journey he had made round the world during the preceding years. This had taken him through the United States, Australia, Ceylon, India and Egypt. In the foreword to this book, *Greater Britain: a Record of Travel in English-Speaking Countries during the years 1866–1867*, which caused a sensation, Dilke wrote:

> The idea which in all the length of my travels has been at once my fellow and my guide . . . a key wherewith to unlock the hidden things of strange new lands . . . is a conception, however imperfect, of the grandeur of our race, already girdling the earth, which it is destined, perhaps, to overspread.

The young world traveller was thinking in terms of 'trusteeship' for races which were not, or not yet, able to cope with the conditions of the modern world; but also, on the grounds of wielding power and preserving the British national character, he set great store on keeping India and the Crown Colonies for Great Britain. On the other hand, he was not much concerned about continuing a close connection between colonies of white settlers and the homeland, even if he did not wish to bring about a separation against their wills. In the case of Canada, he energetically advocated independence. But his indifference to imperial organization at this time was merely the reverse side of his exuberant optimism regarding the Anglo-Saxon race and its civilization, whose widespread dissemination

25, 26 British imperialist publicists: Charles Dilke and James Froude

and world domination he placed far above the traditional standards of national prestige and expansionist policies.

Dilke was later to take a more realistic view of the significance of state power and organization for the advance of the Anglo-Saxon world. In the 1880s, pan-Anglism and imperialism could hardly be viewed any longer as opposites. The former served the latter as an effective ideology. James Froude, whose views on overseas relations also went through several phases, wrote *Oceana, or England and Her Colonies* (1886), in which he made himself the spokesman for those colonists who demanded not only a close union between all the British colonies and the mother country, but in addition a league of all members of the British race. Rudyard Kipling's famous poem 'The White Man's Burden', written in 1899, was addressed to the North Americans, who were about to shoulder an imperialist 'task'. A good many imperialist authors broadened pan-Anglism into Teutonism: a belief in the superiority of the Germanic race and of its world mission. Circumstances permitting, this could mean that, aside from the Anglo-Saxons, opportunities for development might also be granted to the Germans and other Germanic peoples. For example, in his famous Oxford University endowment, Cecil Rhodes provided not only scholarships for Britons from overseas, but also places for Americans and Germans; and these in fact were established. In those days, there was a widespread conviction both in and outside England that the British, the North Americans and (at least from 1870) the Germans were the 'success races' of the nineteenth and twentieth centuries and the leading nations of the future. Their rise and achievements were attributed in part to inherent racial qualities and in part to their Protestantism, which they looked on as the religion of freedom. Protestantism was frequently characterized as the Germanic form of Christendom; thus the religious tendency of the 'Teutonic' peoples was also traced back to racial qualities. The Germanic Protestant principle formed an important component of imperialist ideology from Carlyle to the Conservative author and politician, Geoffrey Drage.

The Anglo-Saxon movement, based on racial or cultural principles, allied itself closely to the British Empire ideology, which was concerned with justifying a system of domination, and which began much further back than the age of imperialism. The awareness of having achieved supremacy of the seas and proven the most successful adversary of Spain, had already tempted poets and publicists in the seventeenth century to draft imperial designs. In patriotic writings from the Baroque era to Lord Palmerston's 'civis Romanus sum' of the nineteenth century, the 'Island Kingdom' took on the guise of a new Protestant Rome or a second Venice, led by an aristocratic *élite*. Images and expressions of speech in currency since the seventeenth century were taken up and adapted by imperialist propagandists in the nineteenth century. But in this, as in other historical ties of imperialist ideology, there is not much more to be seen than ornaments, expressions of an inflated self-consciousness in need of literary, historical, mythical exaltation. The reality of British imperialism was quite imposing enough and raised sufficient problems whose answers were sought in the ideology of empire. It was a matter of finding an overlapping principle and a comprehensive idea for the system of colonies, protectorates and dominions, with the mother country as focal point and metropolis. The main difficulty for Great Britain, as for other large states, was having to deal not only with her own people or related groups overseas but also with peoples and nations of the most varied nationalities and cultures. Besides,

British possessions were extraordinarily diverse in their economic and political functions; they ranged from the Empire of India to colonies of 'white' settlers, and from plantations to trading, naval and military bases. The resulting ideological task could be tackled from two opposite positions. It was possible to evoke a 'consciousness of empire' and its power in order to convince people of its necessity for Britain's greatness, prosperity and independence, for the protection of her naval and economic power, and for her incomparable position in world politics. Or one could start from the welfare of Britain's subjects and those under her protection throughout the world, and emphasize the duties of development and education which had accrued to the British Empire through the assumption of numerous overseas responsibilities. These contradictory imperialist positions rarely appeared in practice to be opposed, but always in more or less pragmatic alignment. Ideologically – and here we are only concerned with ideology – so-called ethical imperialism, with its emphasis on the humanitarian task of the British people, or rather the British race as a whole, became increasingly prevalent. This task consisted in the moral and intellectual elevation of all those people entrusted to British rule until they were ripe for self-government and democracy. Lord Curzon, one of the most outstanding of the British *imperium*'s proconsuls, expressed the conviction that the world had never seen a greater instrument for accomplishing good than the British Empire, while Frederick Lugard, the colonial pioneer, coined the expression 'Dual Mandate' in 1922 to signify on the one hand the immediate task of educating and protecting backward peoples, and on the other hand the future task of securing peace and order in the world.

It was perhaps obvious that when the nations and peoples outside Great Britain had achieved a certain degree of maturity, the concept of domination inherent in imperialism would give way more and more to one of federation and equal rights. Ideology trod the path from empire to commonwealth, which was now perceived as a blueprint for world order and a model for a future international organization embracing all mankind. In Lionel Curtis's publications, the commonwealth idea was delineated as imperialism's highest step. Curtis broadened the imperial idea into an all-embracing concept of mankind which he saw in the light of the *civitas dei*. Yet the beginnings of imperialism lay indisputably in nineteenth-century nationalism. Disraeli's Crystal Palace speech in 1872, frequently taken as the breakthrough of imperialism into public consciousness, was based on the antithesis between cosmopolitan and national attitudes of mind and commended the British *imperium* to the latter.

The European component had already outweighed the overseas one in the empires of Louis XIV and Napoleon I, and on the whole this remained the case in France later on. The greatest expansion of the French colonial empire under the Third Republic took place at a time when the country had temporarily sunk to the level of a second-class European nation. In France too – indeed, especially in France – there was a close interaction between imperialism and nationalism. The population, in so far as they were at all concerned with this aspect of political thought, inclined far more to nationalism than imperialism and had, as a rule, far more interest in home or European affairs than in the colonies. What was the content of French imperialist ideology? If certain circles in Britain or Russia toyed with the idea of constructing a commonwealth of English- or Slavic-speaking peoples, the prerequisites for analogous plans were lacking in France. To win back the French Canadians was purely a pipe dream; although the people of Alsace-Lorraine might be claimed for political, historic and democratic reasons, there could hardly be any claims on linguistic or ethnic grounds; the Walloons desired to remain within the Belgian state. There was certainly a chance of obtaining a leading position among the Latin nations, and tendencies towards Latinism or pan-Romanism did in fact exist. But these trends, confined to intellectual circles, proved much weaker as political realities

27 Napoleon III, Emperor of France until the disastrous defeat of 1871. Many of his ideas carried over to the classical age of imperialism towards the end of the century

than pan-Anglism or pan-Slavism. The Spaniards and Italians cared as little for French guardianship in the name of Latin community as the Dutch or Scandinavians desired German control based on the appeal of Germanism. A belief in the superiority of members of the 'white' or 'Aryan' race, and in a resulting mandate, did play a part among some colonial theorists of French imperialism in the nineteenth and twentieth centuries; it was also current, though less pronounced, among the majority of Frenchmen active overseas – as among all other Europeans in the same position. But this belief never became a constituent part of French imperialist ideology. The determining factor in French, as in British, imperialist ideas was the peculiar tension between considerations of humanitarianism and power politics, the former construed as a Franco-European apostolate of civilization. The idea of France's world mission, especially in the form advanced by the French writer, Edgar Quinet, deserves to be taken fairly seriously as an element in the mood and convictions of intellectuals throughout the country. French imperialism, in so far as it strove for European hegemony, could propose only arguments of security or prestige policies. But in this period such intentions and ambitions were only latent; not until the First World War did they become active again. The nation's imperial energies, which aimed at establishing a France overseas, had already become apparent under Napoleon III. This ruler had ideas of subduing the whole of the Maghreb after the Crimean War, and thus binding his French *imperium* with a *royaume arabe*. At the end of the Second Empire, the author Prévost-Paradol drew a picture of future world politics in which France was allocated its place in Africa. The Roman Empire was constantly held up as a model for France, but such ancient reminiscences had little effect in the end. Wherever imperialism appeared in the colonial sphere, Britain's example was far more decisive. There was a desire to compete with Great Britain and play a role comparable to her position in the world. It may also have been the example of the British *imperium* which led to the increasing prominence of the concept of a protectorate over foreign territories that remained culturally independent and politically semi-dependent

28, 29 Colonialism in North Africa. Algiers, below, was one of the jewels of French imperialism. The port-city of Tangier (painted by Matisse, opposite) was the object of international rivalry

– the associative form of imperialism in contrast to the assimila-
tive form that had originally prevailed. However, the alternatives of assimilation or association were never thrashed out to a
definite solution up to the end of French imperialism. Among
natives in the French, as in all other colonial empires (and not
only in Algeria), the tendency to adopt 'Western' methods
and civilization was countered by a growing will to political

self-assertion which, in the long run, remained unsatisfied by even the loosest forms of political association.

By its name, the German Empire recalls the medieval *imperium* led by German rulers. This *imperium*'s multi-national character was preserved to a far greater extent in the Austro-Hungarian monarchy than in the Hohenzollern Reich, which bore all the marks of a modern national state, apart from the Polish and other very small minorities. In terms of population, economic potential and expansion of state power, however, the German state created by Bismarck had reached a size which, since the 1870s and 1880s, had encouraged imperialist policies inside and outside Europe. The imperialism of Germany, like that of France, contained continental and overseas components, of which the former was the more important. As contemporary publicity media (especially those of the imperialist propaganda associations) unmistakably demonstrate, German nationalism

30 Wilhelm II as an undersized Crusader. This French caricature of 1902 bears the caption: 'The frog who wants to make himself as big as the ox'

31 Buffet-car on the Usambara Railway in German East Africa (1907)

and imperialism were so interwoven that there is no clear-cut distinction between the two. From the very beginning the idea of *Volkstum* was a wider concept which was not limited by the borders of the Hohenzollern state. We are not talking here about dreams of a 'Greater Germany', which never played a note-worthy role in the days of classical imperialism, but about the organization and activation of German nationals abroad. In this case, too, the Reich was much more unfavourably situated than Britain. Whereas Canadians, Australians and New Zealanders were directly governed from Westminster, Germans abroad did not come under the sovereignty of the Reich. In addition, German-speaking populations did not desire any political ties with the Hohenzollern state, and other German groups were either too small or too distant to count for much in power politics. Besides, such plans were never seriously considered by the government at that time. A union between the Habsburg monarchy and the Hohenzollern Reich would have brought the Germans near to a position of continental hegemony. But this was no longer a real possibility since 1866. Nevertheless, individual groups in both states revived the question of Austro-German union when the German Empire passed from its national to its imperialist phase. This happened partly under the banner of common nationality (and its realization would have meant the end of the Austro-Hungarian monarchy), and partly out of the desire to preserve the supranational power complex of the Habsburg state and set up a Central European bloc. In many ways, the second solution would have meant a return to the old Holy Roman Empire of the German Nation or to the former Germanic Confederation, but in a more modern, expanded and, above all, economically determined form. In twentieth-century conditions the leading role in the agglomeration would have gone to Berlin and not Vienna. A continental German imperialism would have had to fall back on the independence of German thought and action *vis-à-vis* western Europe and Russia, a German course of its own already emphasized by the national consciousness of the nineteenth and the early twentieth centuries. Ideologically, this course would place the 'organic-historical' point of view above the concept of natural rights, and constitutionally it would entail a middle way between east and west. This attitude found its most concentrated expression in the 'Ideas of 1914' and the German 'world war' ideology. In his book *Der deutsche Gedanke in der Welt* (1912), the colonial expert and publicist, Paul Rohrbach, advocated the world-wide application of a special German concept of politics and culture. German imperialism's continental orientation was not in conflict with its overseas world political tendency; the two went side by side. This arose willy-nilly from Germany's participation in global economic rivalry and its efforts to obtain 'a place in the sun'. Imitation of Britain played at least as big a role as in the case of the French. There was hardly any idea of a mission to civilize the world tied in with this aspect of German imperialism. In so far as German imperialism reflected upon itself, in the sense of a share in world politics, it moved mainly along the lines of Social Darwinism and was inclined to interpret world history as, in Sombart's words, a 'fight for feeding grounds'. The concept of a world struggle between the Teutons and the Slavs, in which the main burden would be borne by the German Reich, also played a certain role.

V ECONOMICS IN THE AGE
OF IMPERIALISM

32 German caricature
on the state monopoly
of tobacco (1878), an
example of state
penetration of commerce

In his famous tract, *Imperialism, the Highest Stage of Capitalism* (1917), Lenin tried to summarize the imperialist epoch as a social-economic phase within the capitalist era. A 'Western' alternative to the Marxist theory of development, W.W. Rostow's theory of dynamic production in *The Stages of Economic Growth; a Non-Communist Manifesto* (1960), desists entirely from synchronizing the imperialist epoch with any phase of economic history. Instead, Rostow divides those decades in which individual great powers became members of the imperialist movement, into two stages of 'economic rise' and 'maturity', and according to him these periods occur at very different chronological intervals in individual countries. It is certainly true that the imperialist powers appear to us widely varied as to their economic backwardness or advancement. It is futile to try to fix the whole imperialist age in one phase within the numerous theories of business cycles. But this is not to deny that economic crises and booms, and their results, must be accurately noted in a historical description of the imperialist age. In particular, the international economic crisis which began in the 1870s contributed to the origin of imperialism by stimulating the imagination of those caught up in it to find means of escaping from a precarious situation. But neither imperialism nor anti-imperialism expend themselves in economic achievements and opinions; indeed, we can say that the economic side of the phenomenon, for all its importance, does not even constitute the decisive characteristic feature of imperialism.

The first question that arises is how the imperialist era differs from the liberal 'Free Trade' orientation which was dominant

61

up to the last third of the nineteenth century. Classical imperialism is connected in all aspects with the capitalist economic order, as are its opponents, Manchesterism and related trends; it emerges as one possibility among others within the same economic system. To characterize its economics without qualification as Protectionist would be an inadmissible simplification. It is true that Germany introduced protective tariffs on the eve of its transition to imperialism, and several states did the same shortly afterwards. One of the leading imperialist statesmen, Joseph Chamberlain, also fought unswervingly (though unsuccessfully) for the introduction of protective tariffs, for 'Fair Trade' in place of 'Free Trade', during the last phase of his political career. Indeed, it can be said in general that the desire of great power combinations for stronger integration of their territories was frequently coupled with the intention of effecting this by means of a protective tariff, which would consolidate the state or the various parts of the empire. The free trade–protective tariffs alternative, however, also existed outside the realm of imperial politics, and had been argued long before the imperialist age. And the fact itself that Britain maintained the principles of Free Trade during the age of classical imperialism prohibits us from identifying imperialism

33 Bismarck as ringmaster, making Germany's allies jump through the hoop of protective tariffs; a German cartoon of 1879

34 This cartoon from a pamphlet of the Tariff Reform League (1903) shows the rest of the world gathering the fruits of Britain's Free Trade policy

absolutely with Protectionism. Certain well-known imperialists always remained adherents of Free Trade. With some simplification it can be said that not all imperialists were Protectionists, but all Protectionists were imperialists.

There was also a broad tendency towards practical and theoretical neo-mercantilism in the time of imperialism. This can be defined as the desire to build up a powerful national economy augmented by overseas possessions, whose production is geared to the needs of the mother country, while sharply delimiting similar rival systems and even isolating them from the entire home and colonial economy. Just as imperialist world politics were based on the rivalry of the great powers, so the global economy of the period consisted for the most part of competition between national economic bodies, which represented a certain aspect of those great powers and whose dynamics were differentiated according to industrial, agricultural, business and financial impetus. But even the tendency to neo-mercantilism does not explain imperialism as a total phenomenon.

Nor can the economics of imperialism be characterized *only* as the continual increase of overseas markets, the extension of capital exports in particular, the appearance of industrial and commercial undertakings on a world-wide scale, or the continually closer relationship between home and colonial economies. Long before the imperialist age, colonies were highly valued (for example, by English reform radicals) for their economic significance. But what characterizes imperialism with regard to overseas possessions and colonialism is that it gave a political and ideological dimension to colonialism, along with a stronger emphasis on prestige than ever before. As a rule, of course, this did not occur at the expense of economic reason, but the remarkable thing was the accent placed on non-economic viewpoints. And what applies here to the colonial sector of the economy holds for the economy as a whole: what made it imperialist was its intensive cooperation with the state, its assumption of a political character – for example, the granting or refusal of loans to foreign states by private banks on the basis of government directives. The Manchester school's concept of the economy as a phenomenon separate from the life of the state was fought and refuted not only by socialism but also by imperialism.

The economy did not simply pass, under the banner of imperialism, from a cosmopolitan to a national point of view; but its national and imperial consciousness increased, and one can speak of a virtual fusion of economic and state leadership. The idea of a completely independent economy, molested as little as possible by the state, was recognized as doctrinaire and was abandoned. Economic circles no longer desired a state of night-watchmen, assigned nothing but the police task of supporting peace and order so that economic processes could run smoothly, but looked on the state as a powerful and welcome partner. The important entrepreneur functions of the state were valued; attempts were made to do business with the state; and its protection was sought, especially abroad. For its part, the imperialist state often enough used the economy for political

THE FORMULA OF BRITISH CONQUEST

PEARS' SOAP IS THE BEST

REG.ᴰ COPYRIGHT

35 This advertisement of 1887 illustrates the thesis that imperialist competition and the acquisition of colonies had a strong economic link

ends, and the economy put itself at the state's disposal for these purposes. Both state and economy achieved during the age of imperialism a greater range of operation and scope than ever before. It is a sign of imperialism that a phase of economic aloofness from the state was succeeded by one of comparatively optimistic cooperation.

As for the social aspect of this mutual penetration of state and economy, perhaps it may suffice to point out first of all that more and more personalities from economic life, such as bankers, tycoons and business managers, took over the most important state offices. As far as the economic world was concerned, only its leading forces could attempt to bridge the inner alienation

36 Walter Rathenau   37 Viscount Haldane

between economic society, especially industrial society, and the state – more exactly, to overcome the bureaucratic-military, or even feudal, forces who were preferred as leaders and representatives of the state. Indeed this was one of the most important achievements of social history in the age of imperialism. Before the middle of the nineteenth century, it was an exceptional phenomenon for bankers like Necker, Perier or Lafitte in France, or Mendizabal in Spain, to take personal charge of affairs of state. Robert Peel was probably the first member of a business family in Europe to become Prime Minister of a large country. In the age of imperialism, by contrast, bankers and entrepreneurs not only entered politics but attained dominating official positions: Joseph Chamberlain, a manufacturer, rose to be an influential British statesman; Lord Cromer, of the Baring Bros. Bank, was 'proconsul' in Egypt and ranks as one of British imperialism's master architects; the banker Dernburg became German Secretary of State for the Colonies; and Walther Rathenau, even before 1914, paved the way for the political role he was to play during the First World War and in the early years of the Weimar Republic. In France, Charles C. Jonnart, President of the Suez Canal Company and the Saint-Etienne steelworks, took over as

38 Lord Cromer   39 Wilhelm II with the shipbuilder Albert Ballin

Governor-General in Algeria in 1918, and Giulio Prinetti, the
industrialist from Lombardy, was Italian Foreign Minister from
1901 to 1903. In the reverse direction, state officials entered
private industry in order to take up leading positions, or even
to build up big businesses themselves, as the former Prussian
official Alfred Hugenberg succeeded in doing – to say nothing
of the directorships offered to former holders of high office and
senior officers of the armed forces. The old aristocracy was also
strongly represented on these boards of directors. The state
made use of the international relationships of economic leaders
to establish important contacts in foreign political circles: thus
Viscount Haldane's visit to Berlin in 1912 was arranged by
Albert Ballin, the German shipowner and friend of Wilhelm II,
and Sir Ernest Cassell, adviser to King Edward VII and an
important behind-the-scenes figure in Britain. In this period,
many monarchs counted industrialists and bankers among their
circle of friends; indeed, association with such *homines novi* was
in certain respects a criterion for the modern outlook of these
monarchs. The relationships of Edward VII to high finance or
Wilhelm II to the House of Krupp are well known.

The connection between the traditional holders of power
and the new world of the industrial society and technical   67

advance, is well expressed by Richard Dehmel in his poem 'Harbour Festival', which describes the launching of a ship:

> See there: that simple man in the launch,
> Which modestly leaves the teeming quay.
> It is he who brings order to the noisy masses,
> He who earns the private thanks of people living in narrow streets,
> A captain who guides many ships. . . .
>
> Politely he advances through the throng,
> Notables, ladies, gentlemen,
> Policemen, courtiers – all give way. And then
> A Kaiser bows before the Jewish man
> Who conceived the mighty work.
> The officers bow . . .

The poem is about an occasion when Wilhelm II and the powerful Albert Ballin met, and goes on to a general description of the port of Hamburg. In the last stanza Dehmel speaks of the Bismarck Monument at the port:

> Or in the evening, when they go home sooty, dusty,
> They see at the landing-stage, tall as a hero,
> The statesman's statue turned towards the stream,
> And they look up at him as if his shadow robbed their peace,
> And gnash their teeth against his warlike yoke,
> But they're proud of him, yes they're proud.

Cooperation between the state and the economy in the context of imperialist capitalism is frequently interpreted solely as a community of interests, if not worse, between finance and business on the one hand, and the traditional power groups on the other. It goes without saying that such a community of interests did exist under the given social conditions; but the significance of the cooperation between the state and the economy is not completely exhausted by this aspect. Despite all policies of interest and profit, there was also a feeling of

40 Ferdinand de Lesseps, builder of the Suez Canal, with friends in Alexandria (1865)

mutual responsibility between the state and the economy, and the large-scale expansion of the new empires' economic and political strength at home and abroad was welcomed by a wide range of the population, who obtained scarcely any gain from it and who were more concerned with the honour, power and prestige of their country than with profit. The overwhelming participation of middle-class and intellectual circles in the colonial organizations, for example, shows that colonialism could be interpreted as something other than the direct or indirect actions of capital. It had already been shown at the time when shares in the Suez Canal venture were issued that the majority were bought by the French *petits bourgeois* and that large capitalists hardly participated at all. The success of privately financed enterprises abroad was increasingly regarded as a matter of national prestige rather than a mere commercial venture of no further interest to the public. One may well wonder, incidentally, whether prestige and fame are really only fiction, or perhaps actually political realities.

The shift in German 'Reichspolitik', still in Bismarck's time, towards overseas engagements began when the Chancellor 69 proposed to back up the threatened commercial firm of Godeffroy in Samoa. The Reichstag had already adopted protective tariffs, but still no majority could be found at that time to risk taxpayers' money on behalf of a private concern. The 'Mail-Boat Bill' of 1884, which envisaged subsidies to private shipping lines carrying on commercial operations with the Far East, only partly achieved this aim. Later, however, concerted action by official enterprises and private overseas operators became more and more common. Neither Britain nor Germany permitted the failure of any of the private colonial companies which had sprung up during the latter third of the nineteenth century: these were indemnified and their territories taken over.

To quite a considerable extent, the imperialist states put their most powerful banking institutions and economic undertakings at the service of their alliance policies and their political centres of gravity both in and outside Europe. French banks supported Parisian policy by granting enormous loans to the Russian state. In the years before 1914, the rivalry between the Triple Alliance and the Triple Entente in south-eastern Europe and Turkey was carried out no less by means of loan policies, and in this the initiative frequently lay more with the state than the financiers. The state (not as a general rule but in very important cases) also dictated the use of capital and labour, the direction of investment, supplies, and industrial technical undertakings, especially in the sphere of transport. The construction of railways and establishment of shipping lines were central not only to private enterprise, but also to the high political considerations of governments. No contemporary was unaware of the power-political significance of the Trans-Siberian and Manchurian Railways, and no one could have any doubts about the purposes of the intensive building of Russian railways towards the German and Austrian borders. In the case of the partially built Baghdad Railway, which had been started on German initiative and constructed largely with German money, things were more complicated, but it was perfectly clear that this sensational undertaking fell within the general framework of German policy in Turkey. The construction of larger or smaller rail systems in the colonies marked a first culmination in the development of new territories and, at the same time, their political consolidation. And within the dialectics of imperialist challenge and Afro-Asian emancipation, it is characteristic that controversial rail concessions constituted the external cause of the first Chinese revolution in our century. Just as large architectural projects which remained unrealized retain their value as illuminating evidence of ideal and technical architectural history, so railways designed to traverse the globe but never constructed (such as the Trans-Sahara Railway) are instructive in the study of imperialism.

The imperialist system conferred a particularly exalted role on those branches of industry which made technical skills available to the modern power-state. This was primarily true of the armaments industry. Names like Krupp, Schneider-Creuzot, Vickers-Armstrong, Putilov, and Skods had something like a mythical sound to their contemporaries; and even if there were some who cursed armaments manufacturers as criminal profiteers and warmongers, there were others who saw them as the armourers of the nation, whose prosperity and expansion filled them with pride and confidence. In addition to armaments there were many other industries, such as shipbuilding, aircraft (the Zeppelin works in Germany), heavy

41 A view of the Trans-Siberian Railway in 1911

machinery, chemicals and electrotechnics, which, as a result of their business ties with government officials, were unusually close to the imperialist state and its policies, and shared in the patriotic halo demanded by official propaganda. It was nothing fundamentally new when large ships, mines or industrial works were named after the rulers of imperialist nations, their statesmen and generals, but the greater stress laid on this practice was typical of the age: 'Empress Cotton Mills', the 'S.S. Imperator', 'Kaiser Wilhelm der Grosse Mines', etc. When Wilhelm II made an important speech at the Krupp works during the First World War, his intention was not only to make an appearance among the workers but also to use the effective setting of a much-admired giant enterprise. Technical cooperation, as well as personal involvement, between the armaments industry and the armed forces was considerable.

In order to grasp imperialist economy as a whole, we obviously cannot rely on those aspects of its activities which had a propaganda purpose and which took place in public. We have to examine also its secret, underground activities, the

42 Postcard issued on the occasion of the Kaiser's launching of the S.S. *Imperator*

43 The Kaiser visiting the Krupp works on the centenary of the firm, 1912

speculations and massive designs of colonial land acquisition societies, the hunt for concessions, the corruption involved in business success, and the uncontrollable competitive struggle waged all over the globe. The history of imperialism also includes great adventurers, soldiers of fortune, swindlers, shady types and *grands criminels*. One historian may view the development of imperialist economy as a manifestation of the class struggle; another may concentrate on the cut-throat competition or the growth of monopolies, trusts and cartels; while yet a third dwells on the relationships between the economy and the state – but any of these approaches must be based on the unceasing search for technical perfection and increase in production, the continual raising of levels of efficiency among entrepreneurs, engineers, employees and workers, and the irresistible extension of an industrial society as the new dominating social form.

To be sure, these are all things that happened, to some extent, independently of imperialism and could even be discussed without any reference to it. But historical realities make it impossible for us to separate imperialism from the second industrial revolution, the increase in production and the superimposition of a modern industrial society on the former one. A division of the historical process into imperialist power

73

politics and an autonomous economic development would be untenable, indeed nonsensical. The economic-technical change in public life followed with such force that many observers believed they could perceive a recasting of state and politics through the forms and style of economic life. According to Hannah Arendt, one of the main characteristics of imperialism is the penetration of bourgeois capitalist laws of competition and production into politics. One could, however, just as easily draw a parallel between the sharp rivalry of industrial societies – with their political and ideological overtones, identifying themselves with states and empires – and the power struggle among nations which had taken place since the beginning of their existence and continued as before. The question whether imperialism helped to raise standards of living, to spread industrial capacity, to enlarge the arena of professional and special interest associations (from trade unions up to industrial associations) and, in general, to promote the spirit of economic daring, must be answered in the affirmative. State support and incentives carried considerable weight in this. Perhaps it is more correct to say that public opinion, no doubt manipulated by the economy and the state though not altogether created by them, influenced both the political and economic powers in the same direction. This also applies to the gradual spread of a social attitude in imperialist economy.

In comparison with the preceding period, the economy was much more inclined towards the workers' welfare. This did not mean that there was any question of open-mindedness about the workers' independence, still less their partnership in management. There are numerous examples of an almost unbearable paternalism, a combination of social activities on behalf of the workers that were extensive considering the circumstances of the time, and a stern guardianship. Apart from an understanding of social processes, the increasingly close bond between the entrepreneurs and the state certainly influenced their social attitude. To be sure, one could no more speak in that period of a complete social-political neutrality on the part of the state than in any period before or after. But the representatives of the state never completely lost the feeling of responsibility for the population as a whole and for all groups of society, and large industry, because of its close cooperation with the state, was absolutely forced to adapt itself to the state's social policies. Powerful industrialists collaborated in Bismarck's social legislation. Any entrepreneur who felt the need to justify the capitalist system to himself or the general public, or to both, spoke less of his contribution to the social commonweal than of the advantages to his own people, and the greatness and power of the state or empire. Public opinion, however, was not satisfied with the recognition of such advantages merely as an aspect of political economics. It was felt that economic success, which often could be gauged only indirectly, should be supplemented by direct social-political activities, and these began to be used as a measure of the degree to which a people, nation or empire met its responsibilities. Of course

44, 45 Social problems in the age of imperialism. Left, Bismarck is criticized in this German cartoon of 1884 for concentrating on social reform while the colonial powers are expanding their territories abroad. Right, Britain is reminded of her social responsibilities at home

the social-political accommodation of employers can also be attributed to the stronger pressure of the working masses and the intensification of the class war; and it was as part of the same process that the leading groups of industrial society and the social *ancien régime* found themselves together.

It should be emphasized again that a simple 'yes' or 'no' cannot answer the question of the priority of economics, and that the relationship of state politics to the social-economic sphere cannot be explained by the systematic use of a 'super-structure' and 'substructure' theory. If there is one fact that can be taken as proved, it is that neither the First nor the Second World War was unleashed, either directly or indirectly, by 'the economy'. Political-military considerations decided the issue in 1914 as in 1939. Violent differences between American and British petroleum interests, or the commercial rivalry between economic groups of both countries in South America, never led to any serious impairment in the political cooperation of the two nations. On the other hand, the Nye Committee of the United States House of Representatives demonstrated that business interests played a large part in the entry of the United States into the First World War. Although the outbreak of the Russo-Japanese War may be traced back to a financial clique whose interests it suited, almost the whole of Russia's level-headed economic circles were against the adventure. There is no doubt that the economy in general, banks and entrepreneurs played a leading role in imperialist politics, and that the military power of the state was frequently enough employed for the benefit of commercial and banking interests. Britain ordered parts of her fleet to maintain and promote private commercial interests in the Opium War of 1839–42, which there are good grounds for calling the overture to the pre-imperialism of Europeans in the Far East. Anglo-French diplomacy became active in Egypt in order to look after the interests of the Khedive's creditors. The British administration of India had to keep in mind the economic interests of the home country. The opening of Japan by American warships served economic aims; and Great Britain's South African policy carried through the ideas of a man who represented not only the boldest political conception but also the most powerful economic interests. But just as many state actions under imperialism could be listed which bore the exclusive stamp of power or defence policies. Or combinations of state or economic activities could be mentioned which indisputably represent political initiatives and priorities of alliance- or bloc-policies or the consolidation of world-political fronts. In these instances banks and business-houses served merely as political instruments. The 'Panther-sprung' ('panther's leap') to Agadir in 1911 merely used the protection of German economic interests as a pretext. The real issue was to obtain some kind of pledge to be used as a pressure-gambit in the game of political prestige and compensation that was so typical of imperialism. In any case, the idea that the economy of a country must always have been behind its colonial adventures is incorrect; sometimes there was virtually no economic interest at stake at all. Thus today, it is more clearly recognized than formerly that there was a political, as well as an economic, motive behind such events as the French intervention in Tonkin, the occupation of Tunis and, most particularly, the acquisition of areas in Central and West Africa. Such an acknowledged expert as Henri Brunschwig summarizes Jules Ferry's profession of neo-mercantilism as follows: 'It was at this moment, after the conquest and partition of Africa and Indo-China, that economic doctrine justified the policy of expansion, and the economic motor of colonial imperialism began to turn with the political motor.' In many of the military actions undertaken by the great powers, there were no economic factors under debate. It was entirely a matter of capturing support points, providing bunkering ports for the navy, regulating borders and acquiring more favourable military bases.

The interdependence of state and economy in the imperialist age was also made more complicated by the fact that while there was cooperation between governments and commercial concerns, state leaders and high finance, economic empires arose simultaneously which were relatively independent of the states: large private companies with international participation, such as the Suez Canal Company, which eventually came under the exclusive control of Britain but was originally set up on an international basis; the Baghdad Railway; the gigantic Royal Dutch Shell group; or the Union Minière du Haute Katanga. Private companies occasionally attained such importance that the state felt it advisable to make sure of them by obtaining decisive influence: that was why Churchill and Asquith saw to it in 1914 that Great Britain gained a majority participation in the Anglo-Persian Oil Company (later known as the Anglo-Iranian Oil Company). The most unusual example of independent economic expansion during the age of imperialism was the project initiated by King Leopold of the Belgians to achieve the foundation of a sovereign state in the Congo, first by means of scientific-humanitarian activity and later through an international colonial company with primarily economic interests. But even this political-economic *imperium*, in which the grandeur of the conception contrasted with the disgraceful events in the exploitation of the object, could hold its ground for only a little more than twenty years, and the Belgian state had to take it over.

It is not enough to study economic imperialism only as the relationship of the European metropolises to overseas colonies, between which conflicts of interest were never lacking. As already mentioned, the economic, and especially the credit-policy, involvement within the two great rival alliance systems of Europe in the final decades before the outbreak of the First World War was no less significant. The role of foreign, particularly French, capital in Russia is of primary interest. Considerable amounts of German capital also were invested in Russia, and the economic links in the Franco-Russian relationship were as unlikely as elsewhere to produce automatic political results. On the other hand no one can fail to appreciate what it meant that over 53 per cent of Russia's foreign capital

46 King Leopold II of the Belgians (1887)

at the outbreak of the war originated from France, that the Banque de Paris et des Pays-Bas, the Société Générale and the Banque de l'Union Parisienne, along with other French financial institutions, dominated the industry of southern Russia, production in the Donetz Basin and the Russian shipyards on the Baltic and Black Seas. They also controlled the leading Russian banks, especially the Russian-Chinese Bank, and played a decisive role in the foundation of industrial finance companies. Without any doubt the consolidation of the two hostile alliances had its economic side!

The results of imperialist economy, of course, pose simpler and more obvious questions, such as its earning power as a whole, and especially whether or not European overseas investments produced profits. J. A. Hobson took great pains to prove how little British exports benefited from the newly acquired tropical colonies. In the case of France, there is conclusive proof that the economic advantages of her overseas possessions were questionable, and it is well known that the German protectorates, taken as a whole, did not show a profit up to the end of the German colonial era. This can be countered not only by the fact that even a negative economic total balance does not necessarily preclude large profits made by individual groups. Of far more weight is the fact that areas whose development had only just begun could not be expected to show noteworthy returns or have a favourable influence on the domestic economy from one day to the next. Even though the technological civilization of the nineteenth and twentieth centuries promised accelerated development as compared with the past, the transformation of newly acquired territories into economic entities within the framework of empire had to be considered even then as long-term projects. Great Britain, at any rate, could be well satisfied with the economic function of India and the large Dominions within the Empire. And imperialist economy is not to be judged solely on the results of colonial exploitation but also on the results of its service branches, its investments abroad and its share in international companies. Whatever the profits of specific imperialist economic activity, they do not furnish the sole, or even the most important, yard-stick for assessing the universal historical aspects of imperialism. There were not a few cases of imperialist planning, particularly in the early days, when bankers and entrepreneurs, whose attitudes were, in the strictest and narrowest sense of the words, commercial and calculating, held back. However, a high degree of open-mindedness and initiative was shown by those economic leaders whose zest for venture and organization (it has been said that imperialism was fonder of organizing things than making profits) outweighed the profit motive. Men like Cecil Rhodes, George Taubmann Goldie and William Mackinnon, who feared no risks, planned well ahead, speculated boldly and finally conquered, were the types who put their stamp on the imperialist age, and conversely, were brought forth and promoted by it.

The question of the priority of politics or economics with regard to imperialism is a falsely stated alternative. There is a style of thought and behaviour behind both economics and politics, which binds and shapes them, a common attitude of mind and spirit, a relatively unified mode of answering the questions posed by the opening up of the world, the development of technology and economic growth, the population explosion and the rivalry of the world powers. Politics *and* economics began at that time to prefer solutions of large and broad dimensions; sometimes there was a tendency towards the colossal and immense. But were these not almost unavoidable phenomena in the youthful phase of an age of world politics?

VI THE SOCIAL STRUCTURE
IN THE AGE OF IMPERIALISM

An examination of European social history between 1880 and 1914 shows that imperialism as a political era and high capitalism as an economic era cannot be separated from each other. Both are based on the steady and powerful advance of industrial society. It was this that increasingly gave the period its social stamp, even though older social groupings maintained themselves alongside it with remarkable tenacity. The close approach between leaders of state and leaders of the economic class has already been discussed. It was inevitable that this political development should have parallels in the social sphere. Apart from France, where this process had already taken place earlier, the upper middle class first attained its undisputed place at the peak of the social hierarchy during the age of imperialism; this applies at least to leading entrepreneurs, for bankers and merchants had been able to climb quite high even before. Men like Rockefeller, Carnegie, Krupp, Rathenau and Rhodes were now at least as 'interesting' and respected as the bearers of great historical names or leading statesmen, diplomats and soldiers. The traditional *élites* in general accepted and recognized the rise of the upper middle class and their attainment of full equality within the cream of society. Marriages between plutocracy and hereditary aristocracy were increasingly frequent. If one studies the mutual adaptation of both groups, it becomes evident that the upper middle class scarcely developed a special class culture outside its own business and professional sphere, but rather succumbed to a certain process of 'feudalization'. Big estates were frequently purchased and an aristocratic way of life adopted by a generation which could afford and desired leisure. And the top people of industrial society as well as the upper middle class in the monarchical states (the republic of France being the only exception) were all drawn eventually into the aristocracy by means of a comprehensive process of ennoblement. As a rule this meant the entry of a powerful new group into the 'upper crust', to which the bulk of the lower aristocracy did not belong.

An industrial middle class of employees developed between the leading personalities of economic society and the masses of the proletariat. The employees, an unusual social group, could be distinguished at their lowest level only by the nature of their activity, and, according to their salary, often ranked below the better-paid workers; but at their highest level (for example, managing directors) they could already belong to the upper middle class. They could not yet compete numerically with the working population at that time, as they can today, but their social importance increased steadily.

Under high capitalism and imperialism the work-force showed quite different features from those at the beginning of the industrial revolution or even at the middle of the century. It had consolidated itself as a class, had created reliable and effective mutual-interest and professional organizations, and participated in political disputes with growing self-assurance. It was self-evident that that portion of the work-force who were indoctrinated and organized along Marxist lines were anti-imperialist on ideological and doctrinaire grounds. In Britain left-wing liberalism was the main source of anti-imperialist influence on the workers. The fact remained, however, that they profited from the improved economic opportunities offered by imperialism. The ever-increasing diversification in working processes with its increased chances for promotion, the growth of an upper stratum of skilled workers, are characteristic features of the age of imperialism.

The plentiful supply and competition of cheap coloured labour created a specific problem in this period. The racial question as a social-political problem of survival affected exclusively the working class, and led to strong opposition

47 The Ball of Industrialists at Budapest in 1902 is graced by the presence of Emperor Francis Joseph

against the capitalists who were willing enough to use coloured labour in their search for greater profits. The successful struggles by workers in Australia and California against 'yellow competition' are well-known examples; as far as European workers were concerned, it was exclusively the British in South Africa and several other parts of the Empire who were threatened by Chinese competition, and they likewise fought against it with determination. Even in those countries where there was no direct cause for taking a stand, socialist publicists and theorists still felt obliged to debate the problem of how world labour should be divided and the proportion of whites to non-whites in the labour market.

Any study of society during the age of imperialism cannot stop at industrial society in the narrow sense, or at the relationship between employers and workers. Four other groups are of particular importance in the context of imperialism:

Even in France, where feudalism had been more radically abolished than in any other European nation, aristocracy had preserved itself. Although neither united nor decisive, it was nevertheless a power to be reckoned with. Its members, in so far as they chose to serve the state at all, preferred professional careers, such as the armed forces, the diplomatic or colonial services, which were clearly removed from the republican system, and where they could apparently be more useful to the French state than to the Republic. Thus imperialist policy, no doubt unintentionally, created a bridge on which the forces of the *ancien régime* could return to public life by affirming and accepting the new system of power and world politics. The situation was simpler in Britain, Russia, Germany and Italy. A radical break with the *ancien régime* had never occurred in those countries, and its members continued to occupy leading positions in state administration, the diplomatic service, the army and the navy, quite apart from the fact that the Courts were still centres of less or greater political power, and that their social impress was still determined by tradition. Leaving aside those members of the aristocracy who could not see beyond national or regional frontiers, and also the small groups of Russian, Austrian and German nobility to whom any kind of 'adventures' were anathema and who would have preferred, on doctrinaire grounds or for reasons of social egotism, to restore the system of the Holy Alliance, the vast majority of the politically active forces among the *ancien régime* came down heavily on the imperialist side. Here a leading class, which had not yet retired, seemed to find worthwhile tasks; the spirit of the age also had its effect and, finally, a successful imperialist policy seemed the most promising antidote to domestic social revolution. Nor should it be overlooked that colonial and overseas history offers examples of aristocratic attempts to establish settlements, some based on social romanticism but others on realistic experiments.

84

The demographic changes which occurred in the nineteenth century resulted in an enormous population increase not only among the working class but also the middle class. The number of university-trained people in the civil service and the professions increased steadily, as they were constantly replenished from below. It is true that at that time it was not at all easy for sons of the uneducated classes to push their way into academic circles, and for the most part this ladder was not climbed directly from the lowest stratum but from the intermediate class of *petits bourgeois*, who were mainly teachers, lower-grade civil servants, employees and small traders. Jews became increasingly prominent in the learned professions. Anyone successfully completing a university course was given full recognition from then on, and progress in his career did not depend any longer on his origins but much more on his achievement. The situation of women was more difficult, yet in the academic professions a very slow advancement of women in this sphere was also a characteristic of the age. The fact that the principle of achievement, proven first in examinations and later in professional success, had been generally carried through corresponded to the demands of modern society. At the same time (as up to the present day), family tradition and patronage, membership of influential cliques, students' corps or other associations in Germany, going to the right schools and universities in England, as well as political activity, were still very useful, besides the achievement qualification, in getting ahead.

With regard to the professional groupings of the educated middle class we can make a useful distinction between those in state service (senior civil servants, judges, clergymen, schoolmasters) and independent professionals (lawyers, physicians, engineers, architects, artists and, last but not least, journalists). Civil service mentality on the one hand and independence of the state on the other resulted in different political attitudes and activities. As far as political ideas were concerned, the majority of the clergy and of jurists in state service were inclined to be conservative, whereas the other professions showed overwhelmingly liberal and sometimes even radical-progressive tendencies. This is putting it broadly, of course, and does not take into account all the various differentiations.

For the educated middle class during the age of imperialism, however, the opposite poles of 'conservative' and 'liberal' had largely receded and faded, and were often replaced by compromises and even syntheses. In the foreground was a principle which fulfilled and united the majority of this class: their consciousness of nationality. And on this basis many 'academics' found their way to an imperialist conception. Members of the educated middle class as a rule directed the imperialist press and propaganda organizations. The practical tasks which imperialist policy gave to explorers, geographers, doctors, engineers, technicians, and numerous other specialists with scientific or technical university qualifications, certainly did a great deal to win over these groups to the imperialist movement.

No less diverse were the opportunities opened up by imperialism to writers, publicists, journalists, reporters and correspondents. A group of newspaper magnates and publicists, like Lord Northcliffe in England or M.N.Katkov in Russia, were among the most characteristic figures of imperialism. The English journalist, W.T.Stead, who was for a time close to Cecil Rhodes, also belongs to this group. Although despatches from distant theatres of war, instruction through the press on world politics, and collaboration between government and organs of so-called 'public opinion', had begun long before the age of imperialism, it was this age, with its greatly increased demands for information and propaganda, that gave the newspaper world such tremendous impetus and perfected the press as an instrument of influence and control.

The state, the economy, special-interest pressure groups and imperialist propaganda organizations used the instrument of the press, often unscrupulously. Up to a certain point, a section of the press had made itself independent, had developed into a political power factor of the first rank, and pursued policies of its own. A number of press lords and editors even counted among the creators of political events. Statesmen could no longer do without press chiefs and press experts, and found it necessary to keep close contact with newspaper concerns or individual newspapers if they did not wish to become their victims. The enormous expansion of the power of the press had its positive sides: it brought about increased mental agility and understanding of the world, it checked on and arraigned covert political and other practices, it extended intellectual frontiers, it taught and enlightened. But these were counter-balanced by its negative aspects. Many members of the press successfully assumed the role formerly played by fanatical preachers of various denominations: misleading and inciting readers, diminishing their power of independent judgment, warping their decent and rational outlook. No reasonable person doubts the necessity of the press and other communications media as a civilizing influence and the progress they have brought about, but the reverse of this is the fact that com-munications media can also take on terrorist characteristics.

BUREAUCRACY

Although the university-bred higher bureaucracy consisted of the educated middle class and, in the case of individual repre-sentatives, the 'upper crust', its special role demands specific treatment. The monarchs and princes who created the modern state and forced it upon feudal society, used two instruments above all to attain their aims – the army and the bureaucracy. Because of the increasing complexity of administration and jurisdiction, the progressive division of labour in modern society, and the diversification of all public functions, the civil service multiplied, regarding itself as the primary support, custodian and representative of the state.

There was good reason for referring to some countries as omnipotent bureaucratic states in the eighteenth and nineteenth

87

48 The increasing bureaucracy in an imperialist state: post office workers in Berlin (1895)

centuries, even though most of them were provided with a constitution and increasingly assumed traces of modern class society. In the age of imperialism the advanced level of administrative techniques saw to the maintenance of a strong bureaucracy despite counter-forces. The 'classical' government departments were increased by a number of new ones: railways and post, insurance and health services, local government. The growth in the number of civil service jobs was not, of course, restricted to those higher grades which required law degrees. There were hosts of junior and subordinate civil servants, as well as administrative assistants, professional and social groups to whom little attention had previously been paid, but whose numbers alone made them (as today) a political and social factor. In several European countries there was a close personal liaison between the army and the middle and lower bureaucratic levels whose members, for the greater part, were former professional soldiers with long service. Where the relationship between tradition and modernity is concerned, bureaucracy shows a Janus face. On one side it is most closely bound up with technology and the developments towards division of labour; indeed, it supports these. Quite a number of important reforms were brought about on the Continent by active and progressive civil servants. On the other side bureaucracy often identified itself with authoritarian traditions and conservative national attitudes. From the standpoint of social history it is worth noting that, along with the clergy and the officers' corps, the bureaucracy also constituted a professional guild-like element inside modern society, with a strong ethic of its own and an effective discipline, hierarchical in its structure, with distinct ideas on the standards of achievement and conduct which had to be satisfied.

The British Civil Service was offered unique opportunities by the colonial empire, especially India. The practical tasks devolving on British bureaucracy in this sphere created a 'natural' affinity to imperialist mentality. Compared with the extent and effectiveness of the British Civil Service, other countries had much more modest forms of colonial bureaucracy. Of course imperialist convictions were not restricted to those branches of bureaucracy directly concerned with the administration of possessions outside Europe. The more imperialist state policy became, the more the imperialist attitude spread among the bureaucracy – the specifically state-supporting rank of society. Certainly the activities of most civil servants consisted, as

49 The highest post in colonial service: Viceroy of India. This photograph shows Lord and Lady Curzon among Indian notables

before, of routines which had little to do with imperialist attitudes or policies. But the active and daring members of the higher civil service – the decisive and dynamic minorities – were the ones who fulfilled themselves with imperialist ideals and contributed to their realization.

Like the bureaucracy, the military, as an exceedingly important sector of society, poses the question of what distinguished it in the age of imperialism from earlier periods of its history. At all times the power potential of countries has been measured by the strength of their armies and navies. There have been differences, however, in the position of the armed forces within the social structure of the various countries. Whereas the navy enjoyed far more regard than the army in the big seafaring and trading nations, the reverse was naturally the case in the large continental countries whose seafaring and trading activities were more limited. The officer corps traditionally enjoyed a high social standing everywhere, while N.C.O.s and the lower ranks were near the bottom of the social pyramid until the French Revolution. The introduction of compulsory military service changed this decisively. Conscription, compulsory education, and the right to vote formed three pillars of the democratic state, and they were as much the result of social regrouping as a means which served to press on continually the social changes which could no longer be held back. The process of democratization had already advanced considerably in the age of imperialism, and the role of the armed forces at the turn of the century has to be analyzed against this background. The military's modern character has usually been misunderstood because the façade of the army and navy was strongly traditional. The military, in fact, not only retained as long as possible the uniforms and customs of the past, but members of the social *ancien régime* continued to regard the officers' corps largely as their professional domain and it was under their influence that much of the mentality, attitudes, principles of

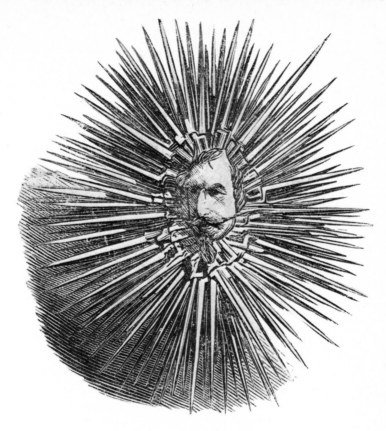

50 This Austrian
cartoon of 1867
comments on the
potential rise of
French *gloire* as the
result of obligatory
military service

leadership and forms of behaviour, which stemmed from before the bourgeois and the industrial revolutions, were preserved. This quite apart from the fact that those who are
concerned with arms develop a mentality basically different
from civilians.

Without the majority of generals and officers becoming
aware of it – indeed, one could say, against the grain of most of
them – the armed forces developed into an instrument of
modernity, with the general staffs as the *avant-garde*. The
military's national educative vocation became equal to its
proper war function on the basis of the general democratization
of society caused by the French Revolution; but this was also a
result of the theories of idealistic German military reformers
at the beginning of the nineteenth century. Although the
idea of the army as a 'national school' could be diverted to

reactionary and militaristic use, it showed a fundamentally democratic tendency, and was certainly meant originally to be entirely democratic and progressive. In the period of imperialism, the belief in a mission of popular education may be ascribed to the German officers' corps as a general conviction. In France an essay by General (later Marshal) Lyautey, *Du Rôle social de l'officier* (1891), pointed in the same direction. British propaganda for the introduction of general conscription did not restrict itself to considerations of power politics and defence; on the contrary, it strongly emphasized the educational aspect.

As a result of the rise in population, armies increasingly took on the features of modern mass organizations. Army command and administration had to adapt itself in many ways to modern management techniques. On the other hand, many forms of political party and special interest group organizations may be explained by the example set up by the military. While the average army officer lived in a world of his own, and armies could actually consider themselves, constitutionally and socially, as a kind of 'state within a state', a very close link-up with the most progressive tendencies of the age had occurred in the economic and technological spheres. A good part of the capacity of technical inventiveness was taken up in the development of war potential, from the introduction of the machine-gun and the submarine to the aeroplane. The whole national economy of every imperialist nation had to adjust itself to military requirements, and vice versa. Thus considerations of a military-political nature also played a role in industrial as well as agricultural production.

An organization of the size and significance of the armed forces could not escape the general ideologizing process dictated by the spirit of the age. By the end of the nineteenth century the military profession and the arts of war had ceased to be unassailable facts of life naïvely taken for granted. The more intellectual military commanders felt obliged to give deeper thought than ever before to the terms of their existence, their mission and their social position – which they tried to defend against attacks by pacifists, left-wing liberals and socialists – whether questioning the right of the armed forces to exist at all, or their political-social structure and practices. Under this pressure, there emerged a very influential military propaganda, which has not yet been systematically evaluated. Outstanding military leaders like Field-Marshal Lord Frederick Roberts, Field-Marshal Colmar Freiherr von der Goltz, General Friedrich von Bernhardi and the later Marshal Lyautey tried personally to influence public opinion by a series of remarkable articles and entered the arena of journalism. An increasingly apologistic and polemical tendency also became evident in the writing of military history, in the works of pro-militarist authors, and not least in the memoirs of war leaders. This deployment of journalistic and literary activity by military men and circles close to them, at any rate helped considerably to promote the esteem of the military, which had not been at all widespread at the middle of the nineteenth century. But it was not until the age of imperialism that serious thought was given to the political education of all members of the army, and particularly N.C.O.s and the lower ranks. There were many reasons for this; not the least was the intention of military leaders to counteract the spread of socialist ideas among those liable to military service.

It was due to the close connection between colonialism and imperialism that colonial troops excited the imagination of the motherland far more than formerly and that they enjoyed increasing prestige. No one could claim that the white (to say nothing of the Asiatic) troops maintained by the British or Dutch East Indian Companies had been held in particularly high regard in their home countries. During the last third of the nineteenth century, however, as the colonial wars – under the aspect of the consolidation as well as the expansion of world empires – achieved a higher rank in the view of the politically interested public, the esteem and popularity of colonial troops and their leaders grew at the same time. Successful colonial commanders like Lord Roberts, Kitchener, Gallieni, Lyautey and Lettow-Vorbeck were virtually national heroes; while Chernayev, Skobelev and Fadeyev, those problematic military exponents of pan-Slavism, made a name for themselves in the Russian colonial wars before their political activities. Defeats such as Adowa, or the fall of Khartoum defended by Gordon, were looked on as national disasters. Even in the early imperialist state of Napoleon III, the large proportion of former colonial officers in leading army positions is striking. General Boulanger began his career as a valiant colonial officer. The participation of 'exotic' units, such as the Spahis and Senegalese, in big military parades in the French homeland was one of the most popular repertory pieces of imperialist pomp. The show of Bosnian troops in Vienna, or the Moorish bodyguard maintained by General Franco for many years, are examples of a similar sentiment. Sikhs and Gurkhas were closely connected with the history, but also with the myth, of the British Empire.

The rise of military prestige in society can also, however, be traced to motives quite different from and more obvious than the colonial one. The foundation of the German Reich in 1871 made a deep impression on the world. This event was rightly connected in the public mind with Bismarck's three successful wars. Furthermore, Bismarck's foundation of the Reich was interpreted as a triumph of the Prussian military monarchy, whose order of state and social system were more strongly related to militarism than elsewhere, and whose effectiveness seemed to be proven. To be sure, this was a somewhat one-sided view. The unification of Germany in 1871 cannot be understood without taking into account the national-liberal movement among the German bourgeoisie. In the simultaneous parallel of Italy, the military component played a far smaller role than in Prussia-Germany, and the centralizing effect was actually even greater there. But events in Germany were regarded (on good grounds) as the more important politically, and, after all, the opinions men form about facts are often more decisive than the facts themselves. In judging the foundation of the German Reich, public opinion at home and abroad inclined very strongly to the view that the rise of Germany – in addition to the genius of Bismarck's statesmanship – could be attributed primarily to military efficiency; and inferences were drawn from this about the importance of the military in the creation, maintenance and expansion of world powers.

In Germany itself, as in all the other great powers, the army became the instrument of imperialist policy, but in its own self-awareness and its behaviour, the mission and *raison d'être* of the national state predominated.

51 This commercial advertisement of 1909 recognizes the prestige of the armed forces in support of imperialism

The public's ideas of imperialism were tied up more with the navy than with the army; and the navy itself, a young and modern institution in Germany, was perfectly aware of its role as the spearhead of German prestige in the world. But the association of naval power with imperialism was by no means an exclusively German phenomenon. Navies had always had a primary importance in the creation and maintenance of empires. However, the results of this, as of many other insights (in themselves correct), reached an almost ideological stage during the age of imperialism. The defence policy of several imperialist countries was completely dominated by the reforms of 'New Navalism' and the large-scale expansion of naval war potential as the central means of aggression among the great world powers. The American Admiral Mahan enjoyed tremendous prestige as historian and theoretician of this point of view. Influential groups were at work in the United States, Britain, France and Germany, who sought not only to press on with the development and construction of one type of warship or another, but also wanted to procure a stronger position in the strategic planning of their states for the navy as a whole. The 'Blue Water School' in England and the 'Jeune Ecole' in France are typical examples of imperialist groupings devoted to naval technology and policy. The 'Blue Water School', in opposition to the 'Bricks and Mortar School', advocated aggressive defence through the navy and regarded the army as a projectile of the navy. The 'Jeune Ecole', like its counterpart in Britain an association of officers, publicists and politicians, also demanded offensive strategy and total trade war. Their efforts were bound up with considerations of foreign policy. Whereas military attachés had previously been assigned by various states to their foreign missions, the additional institution of the naval attaché was effected during the age of imperialism. Although there had been naval visits, demonstrations and reviews before, it was during this period that they reached their greatest extent and their true meaning. For the purpose of making the navy popular, cruises along the coasts ('hurrah-

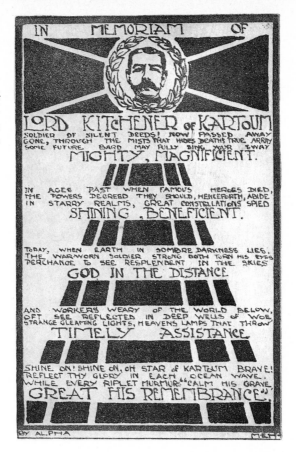

52 A typical memorial to Lord Kitchener, one of the primary imperialist military heroes

trips') were established in Britain from the 1890s. Naval circles played a very active part in French colonial and world policies, while in Russia the navy was more prominent than before in connection with imperialist policy in the Far East. The first Viceroy of the Russian Far East was an admiral.

The significance of naval power for the policies of Great Britain and Germany, and the part it played in the alienation of the two countries, is universally recognized. Whereas the navy had long been at the heart of Britain's national interests, it had first to be made popular in the German Reich. This had a considerable success, first, because of the personal interest taken by Kaiser Wilhelm II, and also because of the extremely astute propaganda work of the central naval agencies, headed by the office of the later Grand Admiral Tirpitz, who worked fruitfully with the Flottenverein (Naval Association) in order to win over public opinion. The Flottenverein had been preceded by the foundation of the Navy League in Britain in 1895. In all the great powers, the navy became the pet of consciously imperialistic circles and this had some effect on the navy's position in society. The appearance of sailor-suits for boys and sailor-blouses for girls is an example of the navy's popularity; this fashion was even to outlive the age of classical imperialism in the European states, in North America and Japan. Prior to 1914 the air force was too new and still too much in the experimental stage to capture the attention of the public as the navy had succeeded in doing. It was only during the war that the airman secured a leading place in the military caste and indeed in society.

Finally, the imperialist need for expansion gave a number of officers the opportunity to enlarge their knowledge of the world, as members of military missions and advisory staffs, as commanders and instructors in foreign services, as military partisans acting independently of their own governments, often disavowed by them and yet in contact with them. These men, once they returned home, frequently emphasized the military and strategic aspects of world politics and promoted the imperialist movement in their countries.

53, 54 The vogue of sailor-suits applied to ordinary children as well as to the British royal family

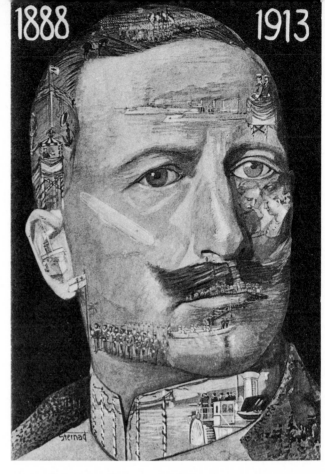

1888 1913

55 The events of Wilhelm II's reign reflected in his portrait. The emphasis is clearly on military and naval power

The social tableau of the age of imperialism would be in-complete without mention of another significant characteristic of the period: the powerful growth of associations and organizations, the enduring establishment of great pressure groups. Here we are concerned less with mass movements, which had long existed, than with the perfected organization of special interest groups, assisted by all social techniques known at the time and the deliberate use of mass-communication media. Of course the appearance of large associations was not something utterly new. There had been the League for the Abolition of Slavery, the Free Trade movement, Cobden's National Anti-Corn Law League, the American caucus system, and the rise of the trade unions, not to speak of the models offered to modern associations by the structure of churches, orders and sects. But the typical feature of this age was the almost complete extension of an influential system of associations over professional and mutual interest groups. Employers and employees, trade and industry, but also teachers in all kinds of schools and the independent professions – all combined in professional organizations and special interest associations. Besides these, there now developed the new imperialist propaganda organizations for the colonies, the army, the navy, and for imperialist policy generally: tight structures, exploiting the refined arts of advertising, extremely aggressive in tone and in the methods for achieving their aims. Non-government-service Europeans in the colonies or in areas outside Europe frequently created agitation lobbies, such as the French *colons* in Algeria, or the Anglo-Indian Association. These groups achieved their full political dimension only through their cross-connections with the press and parliaments. One could even go so far as to speak of infiltration of the press and the political parties (or of the parliamentary groups) by representatives of these lobbies. The inter-connection in the parliamentary groups between supporters of colonialism, Protection, agricultural interests and many other lines of policy deserves particular attention. The formation of parallel organizations with strong influence on legislative assemblies and the press can be observed in the area of religious communities. A new type of social species emerged as leaders or exponents of these organizations: syndics, managers, general secretaries, but also minor propagandists, agents and lobbyists, who were often active not only within their own associations but also in journalistic and parliamentary circles. Thus, in addition to the industrial manager, the association manager – the functionary of parties and leagues – came forward as a weighty figure in the social-political life of the age of imperialism. The functionary is largely the object of unfriendly public opinion, but it should not be forgotten that modern pluralistic society could not exist without him.

VII ORGANIZATIONS OF THE IMPERIALIST MOVEMENT

56 Motto of the German
National Shop Assistant's
Association

Like nationalism, imperialism is a movement – that is, it does not stop at doctrine and isolated literary and journalistic expression. On the contrary, the imperialists grouped themselves into specific circles, committees, associations and leagues. They tried to influence public opinion and took political initiatives. They pressed for power in the state and, even if they never achieved complete domination in the government of any country, they still succeeded now and then in wielding decisive influence or at least in obtaining strong positions in state leadership.

As in the case of all other movements, the systematic development of theory and practical action was preceded by the preparatory efforts of scholars, writers and publicists, who intellectually dug the soil for the new seed, and produced an atmosphere favourable to a certain mode of conduct. Long before the amalgamation of imperialist groups was successful in Britain or the government began to act on imperialist lines, Thomas Carlyle preached new ideas closely related to imperialism and Charles Kingsley tried to strengthen the awareness of empire and power. In Russia individualists like the historian Pogodin, the historical philosopher Chomyakov and the diplomat Tyuchev proclaimed the programme of a political pan-Slavism in journalistic, scholarly and poetic forms even before its organization could be tackled at the end of the 1850s. If the prophecies of individual intellectuals happen to match the general contemporary political experience, the chances for the rise of a new movement improve considerably. Experiences of the kind likely to promote imperialism could be disappointment over military or diplomatic defeats; the realization that economic expansion could surmount certain obstacles only with the support of state power; or that the best way to hold one's ground in difficult situations was through the consolidation of power politics. A movement may often be fathered rather by hope than by particular experiences; it may be fostered less by the weight of facts than by the inventiveness resulting from an awareness of crisis; it may emerge out of an attempt to master a critical situation, or the accurate perception of unusual political and commercial opportunities or, again, the urge to imitate others' successes.

Thus the British Empire as a whole, or even the superior British Navy, absolutely fascinated numerous Frenchmen and Germans; we know who were the British models for French publicists like Leroy-Beaulieu, Rambaud, Siegfried or the German colonial pioneer Carl Peters. Conversely, the founding and strengthening of the Hohenzollern Reich, and the Prussian-German Army, made a strong impression on a great many Englishmen and was one of the reasons they began to pursue an imperialist course in power politics and military policy. The oppression of the Bulgarians by the Turks gave rise to the establishment of so-called 'Slav Committees' in Russia after the 1850s; these started as welfare and assistance groups, but soon turned into centres of pan-Slav agitation. The attacks of the Jamaica Committee against Eyre, the Governor of Jamaica, because of his severe measures, provoked adherents of a power-conscious and rigorous policy, such as Carlyle, Tennyson and Froude, into starting an Anti-Jamaica Committee which not only supported Eyre but also affirmed in general the principle of imperialist policy. The Alldeutscher Verband (Pan-German League) of 1890 resulted from dissatisfaction with the Zanzibar-Heligoland agreement. Apart from those groups and associations which were founded *ad hoc*, there were societies in all the larger states which gradually evolved an imperialist attitude because of their practical and specialist dealings with European and overseas problems. In this category, the significance of the geographical societies in Great Britain, Russia, France and

57 John Millais' portrait of
Thomas Carlyle, intellectual
purveyor of imperialist
ideology

Germany can scarcely be overestimated. A study of the themes
of the lectures and publications of these societies shows how
profoundly they pressed to turn theory into practice, and to
what extent these were intellectual laboratories, whose
members considered and discussed many of the things they
wished to see realized. Men of learning and practical experts
met together, and those with overseas experience were only
too glad of the opportunity to send up trial balloons in the
geographical societies' comparatively informal atmosphere.
There was also no lack of cross-connection with interested
economic circles and chambers of commerce. A characteristic
example of the combination of scientific geography and
economic journalism at the service of imperialism in Germany
was Robert Jannasch, founder of a Verein für Handelsgeographie
und Förderung deutscher Interessen im Ausland (Society for
Commercial Geography and the Promotion of German
Interests Abroad) in 1878, which had been preceded by other
European foundations, such as the Société de Géographie Commerciale in Bordeaux (1874). Jannasch had revised a book by
the economist Wilhelm Roscher, *Colonies, Colonial Policies and
Emigration*, and published and edited the journal *Export*. The
British Royal Colonial Society (later the Royal Colonial
Institute), founded in 1869, was an example of the association
of scientific and political discussion. The carrying over of
scientific interests into economic and political concerns

assumed vast dimensions in the undertakings of King Leopold II of Belgium, out of which the problematical 'Belgian Congo' finally emerged.

But the geographical societies were not alone in this field. Numerous 'study groups' and 'research committees' with an economic accent were working in the same direction. Missionary societies were able to give a direct (and even more an indirect) drive to the imperialist movement. Certainly the ultimate aims of Christian missions did not coincide with those of imperialism, and the missionaries often came into sharp conflict with the white settlers, for example in South Africa. But all denominations were aware of the protection afforded to missionary societies and religious orders by the white powers; in many instances they desired government intervention. We know that from time to time the Evangelical movement had a strong influence on the Colonial Office in London, though this was in no way with imperialist intent but rather to encourage missionary work and participation in humanitarian efforts. Catholic circles (Louis Veuillot) had a stimulating effect on the colonial policies of France and the Evangelical theologian Frederic Fabry on those of Germany. Missionary history – especially in the Far East but also in Africa and other non-European areas – offers numerous examples of a community of interests and action between missions of all faiths and the imperialist policies of the European states. The undertaking of protectorates for religious minorities in non-Christian countries by the great powers since the eighteenth century should be seen as the first step to imperialist policy, and there was certainly no inclination to renounce this tool during the age of imperialism itself. A few examples of the cooperation between imperialist power politics and clerical missionary policies are the missions of the Orthodox Church among the Asiatic pagans and the Persian Nestorians; the part played by John Baptist Anzer, the Catholic missionary bishop, in the taking over of Kiaochow on lease by Germany; and, in particular, the activities of Cardinal Lavigerie, an important

CIVILIZATION
Misgovernment
Mismanagement
Dissymulation
Iron Duke (again)
Turkish Bonds
Foreign Troops
Murder
Frauds
Starvation
&c &c

Daily Telegraph

New York Herald

RUM

MISSIONARY PIE

THE NEW AFRICAN MISSION.

Rev. Mr. Fun:—"THIS, DEARLY BELOVED BROTHER, IS OUR CIVILISATION. A TEMPTING PICTURE, IS IT NOT?"

58 Anti-imperialist and anti-
missionary cartoon of 1875

Prince of the Church, in Algeria and of the missionary order of
the White Fathers which he founded. These organizational
beginnings and indirect incentives to the imperialist movement
were followed by specifically imperialist bodies: the great
propaganda organizations and pressure groups. A distinction
must be drawn among propaganda organizations between those
which had a comprehensive object in view with the intention
of promoting patriotic power politics in every sector of public
life, and others which set themselves specific tasks within this
general framework. The Imperial Federation League (1884),
which was succeeded by the British Empire League, and the
Primrose League (1883) were among the associations working
towards an imperialistic orientation of politics as a whole: the
former, a non-party group with leading Liberals and Conservatives at its head; the latter, an exclusively Conservative imperialist body which developed into a mass organization in the first

105

decades of its existence. In Germany, the Alldeutscher Verband (Pan-German League) took on the task of strengthening the national power position by simultaneous campaigns in the spheres of nationalism and colonialism, world and defence policies. Numerous other associations with more limited objectives were added to organizations of this nature. The Federal Union Committee aimed at an approach between the British homeland and the colonies in legislative and administrative affairs, while the United Empire Trade League, and later the Tariff Reform League worked for a comprehensive customs and trade agreement within the Empire. The Royal Colonial Institute and the Imperial Institute, each in its own way, strove for imperialist unity between Britain and the colonies. The Comité de l'Afrique Française applied itself to cultivating pro-colonial ideas among the French public; and the Deutsche Kolonialgesellschaft, a fusion of two earlier organizations, carried out corresponding propaganda in Germany. The Flottenverein (Navy League) and the Wehrverein (Army League) agitated for an open-minded attitude among the population towards military preparedness in Germany, and similar action was undertaken in Britain by the more scientific Navy Records Society (1893) and the very influential Navy League (1895). The National Service League under Lord

59 Vignette of the Navy League, with a portrait and quotation of Nelson (1898)

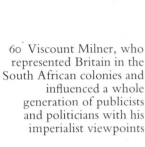

60 Viscount Milner, who represented Britain in the South African colonies and influenced a whole generation of publicists and politicians with his imperialist viewpoints

Roberts made propaganda for universal conscription in Great Britain. An Empire Economic Union assisted British economic interests under imperialistic auspices. The Slav Committees in Russia tried to establish connections between the Tsarist Empire and the Slav nations and nationalities outside Russia, while the Verein für das Deutschtum im Ausland (League for the Preservation of German Cultural Identity Abroad) sought to strengthen German national groups outside the Reich. Finally, there were propagandistic cultural organizations in all the large states. The functioning of the mass organizations presupposed the existence of strong leadership cadres which occasionally won great political influence. Independently of the large associations, leading theoreticians and practical experts could also join in smaller circles and 'schools', which were often collected round a publicity organ. A classical example of this sort of group was Lord Milner's 'Kindergarten' and the circle connected with the journal *Round Table*.

These are only a fraction of the imperialist associations and groups which had standing and influence. As attempts to form and organize 'movements', they had precursors, some of which have already been mentioned. One can add to them associations with purely national and non-imperialist aims, such as the Società Nazionale in Italy and the Deutscher Nationalverein of

1859 – organizations whose structure the imperialist associations took over. Perhaps the greater frequency with which such associations sprang up, the intensity of their recruiting, and the modernity of their propaganda methods, are characteristic of the age of imperialism. The cultivation of public opinion through their own publicity organs, while at the same time infiltrating the national press, reached proportions scarcely equalled in the past. Among the members of these organizations, there already appeared, in addition to the journalists employed full-time by the associations, those functionaries, already mentioned, who form one of the most remarkable professional groups of our time. The gamut of publicity work ranged from the traditional unveiling of memorials and banquet-speeches to organized mass events (especially mass rallies), the unleashing of storms of addresses and petitions (these, of course, had also taken place long before imperialism), and the introduction of remembrance days (such as Trafalgar Day or Empire Day). The Great Exhibition held in London (1851) and those which followed it provided models for the large empire and colonial exhibitions in London or the Slav-Ethnographic Exhibition in St Petersburg, in which economic programmes were diverted into political and imperialist channels. The organizational and propaganda peculiarities of Russian imperialism, which were bound up with pan-Slavism, came to light for the first time at the Slav Congress of 1867 in Moscow, in the political emphasis on the cult of St Cyril and St Methodius, and in the highly developed relations of Russian scholars and national societies with their Slav opposite numbers abroad. Another specifically Russian feature was pilgrimages by non-Russian Slavs to Moscow; visits by Princes of the Orthodox Church from countries outside Russia; receptions of Slav royalty, such as the Princes or Kings of Serbia and Montenegro who were regarded as kith and kin. Eventually the ruler of Montenegro succeeded in bringing about a family link with the Russian dynasty. This event, though it appeared to be purely dynastic, is also to be seen as thoroughly in line with pan-Slav and imperialist

61 Souvenir of the centenary of Trafalgar (1905) ▶

A Souvenir of

TRAFALGAR.

1805=1905

perspectives. The accelerated democratization of political life and its inherent public claims resulted in increased involvement of heads of state in speechmaking, state visits, receptions and official tours, all of which were exploited for imperialist aims. Celebrations of special anniversaries, especially Queen Victoria's Royal Jubilees in 1887 and 1897 were made use of for imperialist demonstrations, and provided opportunities for holding Colonial Conferences (later Imperial Conferences).

The question of which social groups supported the imperialist movement and from which side the initiative stemmed, cannot be answered by referring simply to interested capitalist circles. Money certainly flowed into the treasuries of the imperialist propaganda associations from industry, from commercial houses and banks, and the economic interests of many influential groups of entrepreneurs coincided entirely with the political and journalistic aims of imperialist agitation. Much has been written about these facts and about the leading roles taken in imperialist organizations by individual aristocrats, generals, admirals, governors, colonial officers and civil servants, traders and shipowners. In contrast, insufficient weight has hitherto been given to the consent of the educated middle class – the intelligentsia – and to their active participation in the imperialist movement. The members of this social class could not have expected any profit worth mentioning even if all their country's imperialist plans had been totally successful. As a rule, they could not count on having a say in political-military decisions and economic planning. It was mainly their conviction of the necessity of power politics, and often a belief in their country's world mission, that made them support the cause of imperial- ism. A very large proportion of professors and teachers in universities and secondary schools, senior civil servants and independent professional men with academic training, stood in the imperialist camp from the beginning of the twentieth century at the latest. As far as support for imperialist aims by the officer corps is concerned, a 'natural' professional interest was involved. To be sure only few officers and generals on active service had time or opportunity to engage in imperialist propaganda; but all the more were the numbers of retired (but still active and enterprising) officers, admirals and generals who offered their services to imperialist organizations. Finally, the participation of Church circles in the imperialist movement should not be overlooked; this was by no means confined to the mission field. The Anglican Church, the Russian Orthodox Church, and the established Evangelical Church in Germany were so closely bound up with the politics of their particular countries and ruling houses that they could hardly do anything but welcome every success achieved and justify every success sought after. Imperialist successes gained by the state were regarded by Protestant circles in Britain and Germany as successes for the cause of world Protestantism or, in the case of the German Reich, as a consolidation of the 'Evangelical Empire'. The laying of the foundation-stone and the dedication ceremony of the Evangelical Church of the Redeemer in Jerusalem provided the ostensible excuse for the two Eastern pilgrimages of Wilhelm II, mock-heroic manifestations of young German imperialism. In Russia, high-ranking Orthodox clergy were closely linked with the Slav Committees; every increase in the Orthodox Tsar's power or that of his state must also benefit their Church. In France, Catholicism was confronted with specific problems. The tense relations between the Catholic Church and the Third Republic are well known; if there was one area of political action, however, in which the anti-clerical state and the inimical Church could still work in harmony, it was that of French imperialism and particularly colonial policy.

Such a powerful movement as imperialism was bound to make itself felt in party politics and in parliamentary life, in the form of either associated action across party lines, or the extensive or total identification of existing parties with the imperialist programme, or the creation of imperialist parties. The colonial groups in the French Chamber and Senate and the British Parliamentary Navy Committee are examples of inter-party alliances. In Britain the Conservative Party declared itself explicitly for imperialism; the Liberals were divided into an imperialist and an anti-imperialist wing. When Joseph Chamberlain and his friends seceded from the Liberals and re-formed as Liberal Unionists, an imperialist party *par excellence* came into being. The Union between England and Ireland was defended or opposed partly on its own merits, but it was also regarded as a criterion and a symbol of the mother country's will to maintain the unity of the Empire. In France, a 'Colonial Party' composed of various shades of opinion was started in the Chamber of Deputies and in the country during the last decade of the nineteenth century. The majority of French deputies, apart from the socialists, could be won round to an armaments policy and imperialist foreign policies within a European

63 Poster for Francis Joseph's Jubilee celebration in Vienna, 1908

62 French caricature of Wilhelm II's journey to Turkey, Palestine and Jerusalem in 1898

framework. The same applied to Germany, where the National Liberals and Free Conservatives acted as the *élite* of imperialism. With a few exceptions, they could generally count on the German-Conservative Party (Deutschkonservative) to pursue imperialist aims, while the Centre Party and the Liberals (Freisinn) could only be won over from case to case. The blocs created by Bismarck to approve the army estimates, and, even more, the Bülow bloc, formed to facilitate imperialist naval and colonial policies, are examples in Germany of supra-party parliamentary cooperation in the service of world power politics. The 'Fatherland Party', organized in Germany as a 'super-party' during the First World War and intended to force the

113

conflict to a victorious conclusion as well as encourage absolute endurance, had an explicitly imperialist character. The Russian Octobrists, who corresponded closely to the German National Liberals, advocated the most decisive imperialist programme, which also found support in other quarters. The imperialist front in Italy ranged from Giolitti's Liberals to Corradini's Nationalists.

If public opinion and political life in the European great powers were saturated everywhere in the spirit of imperialism, it could not be expected that heads of state, ruling houses and governments would be exceptions. From Alexander II onwards, the Russian Tsars encouraged and supported pan-Slavism, as well as all other imperialist tendencies, though this had to be done with a certain discretion as far as pan-Slav efforts were concerned. Queen Victoria always encouraged her ministers whenever they pursued imperialist policies and she herself was responsible for a number of initiatives in that direction. For her successors, the creed of empire, in a more or less imperialistic sense, became a matter of course. Wilhelm II was regarded in Germany as the 'Industrial and Naval Emperor', as Friedrich Naumann called him. He signalized all too stridently Germany's entry into the imperialist era and symbolized through his behaviour and interests the new world-political course which was put into effect after Bismarck's retirement. Italian imperialism could always count on the House of Savoy's compliance. Some European monarchs may have developed more understanding of imperialism as a modern ideological and practical movement than others – but scarcely any of them was quite free of the instinct to extend his power. An increase in the power of one's own country within and outside Europe would, they thought, inevitably benefit the splendour and prestige of the dynasty.

Among the Prime Ministers of the period, Disraeli, Rosebery and Ferry were also leading imperialist politicians. But it is more significant that, apart from Gladstone's last cabinets, none of the relevant European governments was outspokenly anti-imperialist after the 1880s. Even Gladstone, the opponent of imperialism, had to make considerable concessions as a practising statesman to the political realities dictated by imperialism. There were certainly many cabinet members who had no interest in a policy of expansion or were opposed to it in principle; but their influence was more than balanced by the policies of their colleagues who were pro-imperialist and who had more efficient means of influencing public opinion at their disposal. By their very nature, the ministries of war, naval affairs and colonies formed centres of imperialist initiative within the cabinets. Influential men from the colonial administrations, the army general staff and the admiralty were behind their ministerial heads. Chamberlain and Hanotaux as ministers for the colonies, Etienne as Secretary of State for the Colonies, Tirpitz as Secretary of State for the Reichsmarineamt (German Naval Office) were all impressive exponents of imperialist policies. At the same time heads of other departments could exercise authoritative influence in this direction, for example, Count Ignatiev as Russian Minister of the Interior. In a world of increasing democracy, it became taken for granted that

64 Gabriel Hanotaux 65 Joseph Chamberlain

imperialist statesmen would take a great many of their decisions not in the style of independent cabinet policies but, on the contrary, in cooperation with the parliamentary groups, parties and organizations that were closely connected with them. State leadership frequently financed the imperialist propaganda organizations and supported them in other ways; they were also often used as instruments of state policy, and assigned tasks of agitation and propaganda which official circles neither could nor wanted to carry out. These vast associations, however, were still far from being merely automata receiving orders, like the mass organizations in totalitarian states. There were many conflicts between the policies of imperialist governments and those of imperialist associations, which are easy to account for in view of the heterogeneity of both spheres. There had always been strong opponents of the pan-Slavs in the Tsarist government; the pan-Germans never succeeded in gaining decisive influence over official government policy; and from time to time there were even differences of opinion and friction between the closely cooperating Reichsmarineamt and the Flottenverein. Nevertheless, in the last decades before the First World War, there developed in general a well-functioning interplay between independent social initiatives and official statesmanship in the field of imperialist policy.

66 Admiral von Tirpitz

VIII THE ANTI-IMPERIALIST FRONT

In several countries imperialism emerged to a great extent as a counter-movement to the concept of the primacy of economic factors and abstinence from power politics. It never succeeded, however, in completely vanquishing its opponents anywhere. Economic liberalism and, on the other hand, radical humanitarianism asserted themselves throughout Europe as powerful forces; they answered the challenge of imperialism with subtle argumentation and intensified agitation.

A reading of the proceedings of the British Parliament, the German Reichstag, or the French Chamber of Deputies shows how heavy the fire was that Free Traders and anti-colonialists directed incessantly against the imperialist policies of these states. Left-wing liberalism, in so far as it was doctrinaire, put up a strong fight against armaments and power policies, the acquisition of non-European territories, the establishment of naval bases and, above all, the retreat from its economic principles. This defensive struggle produced its own pressure groups: special interest organizations of the economic circles dedicated to Free Trade, who had considerable influence on party politics. Certain English theorists, who subjected imperialism to searching criticism in their programmatic works, attained greater international renown than functionaries of anti-imperialist leagues or parliamentary champions of left-wing liberalism; their convictions still hold good today among middle-class and other leftists – indeed, they have recently gained (or regained) even greater currency.

The writers concerned were specialists in political economy or sociology, and their starting-point was always an analysis of economic and social life. John A. Hobson (1858–1940) probably wielded the greatest influence; his book *Imperialism*, first published in 1902, has been reprinted many times up to the very recent past, and will be discussed in a later chapter. Another writer of major influence was Leonard T. Hobhouse (1864–1929), a political journalist and professor, who mounted a scientific onslaught on two fronts against the old Manchester school of *laissez-faire* individualism and the neo-mercantilism advocated by the imperialists, both of which he desired to replace with constructive liberalism. In the political field he argued the case for jurisdiction through arbitration, disarmament and radical democracy in home and foreign affairs. His criticism of imperialism is most effectively set down in the book entitled *Democracy and Reaction* (1904). Historically correct, he begins by dealing with the liberal roots of imperialism, particularly its origin among the Colonial Reformers. Unfortunately, their programme was distorted; the theory and practice of imperialism are two different things.

A political theory must be judged not only by its profession but by its fruits. What then, were the fruits of Imperialism, *i.e.*, of the actual policy urged by Imperialists and defended on the ground of Imperial necessity? Did it, for example, give us peace? On the contrary, the perplexed observer, looking vainly for the British peace which was to be, was confronted with an endless succession of frontier wars, some small, some great, but all ending with the annexation of further territory. Under the reign of Imperialism the temple of Janus is never closed. Blood never ceases to run. The voice of the mourner is never hushed. Of course, in every case some excellent reason has been forthcoming. We were invariably on the defensive. We had no intention of going to war. Having gone to war, we had no intention of occupying the country. Having occupied the country provisionally, we were still determined not to annex it. Having annexed it, we were convinced that the whole process was inevitable from first to last. On each several occasion we acted purely on the defensive, and on each several occasion we ended by occupying the land of our aggressive neighbours. Such is the fiction still solemnly maintained. The naked fact is that we are maintaining a distinct policy of aggressive warfare on a large scale and with great persistence, and the only result of attempting constantly to blink the fact is to have introduced an atmosphere of self-sophistication, or in one syllable, of cant into our politics which is perhaps more corrupting than the unblushing denial of right. . . .

The observer who was not content with fair professions but wished to know in all seriousness whither he was being led, found set before him two deeply-contrasted pictures of Imperialism – the Imperialism of promise and the Imperialism of performance – the one based on the conception of the Empire as built up by Liberal statesmen, the other on the policy of Empire as shaped by a generation of Imperialist statesmen. . . . Little by little it became clearer that the new Imperialism stood, not for a widened and ennobled sense of national responsibility, but for a hard assertion of racial supremacy and material force.

67 Anti-colonial French cartoon (1902), bearing the caption: 'While waiting for reinforcements let's do a spot of work ourselves'

Both Hobhouse and Hobson saw a special danger in the effects of a brutal foreign policy on home policy. In an imperialist system, it was not only the freedom of weaker nations that was jeopardized, but also that of the states wielding power. As an example of this, Hobhouse cited the absence of urgent social reforms under British Conservative governments between the 1880s and 1904. Moreover: 'the absorption of public attention in foreign affairs paralysed democratic effort at home'. A 'reaction against humanity' spreading throughout civilization, as Hobhouse put it, as well as Hegelian philosophy, were responsible for the unpleasant development of imperialism. He was referring to Social Darwinism, the biological interpretation of social data, the substitution of concepts of race and heredity for those of freedom and equal rights.

> Evolution is conceived as a vast world process in which human will and human intelligence play a subordinate, and, in a sense, blind and unconscious part. The great biological forces work themselves out without any conscious contribution from the organisms with which they sport. . . . The most intelligent actions, the widest schemes, the noblest ideals of men are produced by physical causes of which they are unconscious, and have biological effects which bear no relation to the intentions of the agent concerned.

He approved of a federal commonwealth based on democratic principles in home and foreign policy:

> Democracy may be reconcilable with Empire in the sense of a great aggregation of territories enjoying internal independence while united by some common bond, but it is necessarily hostile to Empire in the sense of a system wherein one community imposes its will on others, no less entitled by race, education, and capacity to govern themselves.

His last word on questions of international politics was a system of international law opposed to reactionary theories of world-empire. Hobhouse and his direction of thought managed

THE IMMENSE AND
BROODING
SPIRIT STILL
SHALL QUICKEN
AND CONTROL
LIVING HE WAS THE
LAND AND DEAD
HIS SOUL SHALL BE
HER SOUL

68, 69 Cecil Rhodes, the great hero of
imperialism. Right, his memorial in
Capetown. Above, French cartoon
showing his 'funeral monument raised
by the Boer collection'

to gain a strong position in the London School of Economics.

Men like the philosopher and sociologist Herbert Spencer, the journalists and politicians Leonard Courtney, Henry Noel Brailsford and numerous others must be mentioned alongside Hobson and Hobhouse. All were representatives of an evolutionary progressivism, heirs and executors of British radicalism, who refused to acknowledge imperialism as an intermediary stage on the road to the international organization of mankind and to a social order striving for the greatest possible welfare for *all*. The majority of them had been resolute opponents of the Boer War. As time passed these radical liberals increasingly found a positive bond with the trade unions and the labour movement. While British imperialism, for its part, was putting out feelers through a few Fabians and other theorists towards

121

socialism within the country, the ideas of writers like Hobson and Hobhouse had a greater *de facto* success in the British labour movement. Not only the British, but the entire international socialist movement ultimately proved more successful in the fight against imperialism than orthodox Free Traders or radical middle-class intellectuals.

Neither the ideologists of Marxism nor the Marxist movement had started out primarily opposed to imperialism. Their struggle had begun before the start of the imperialist movement, and their first target was the existing liberal economic and social order. But neither Marxist theoreticians nor those closely allied with them found it difficult to integrate imperialism ideologically, to interpret it (in Lenin's words) as the 'highest stage of capitalism', or to extract from imperialist policies an inexhaustible supply of material for agitation. Leading Marxists like Lenin, Hilferding, Rosa Luxemburg, Kautsky and Bukharin carried the liberal left-wing criticisms of imperialism a stage further and intensified it in the spirit of their own ideology. What carried weight in political practice was the fact that, along with the socialist parties and most of the trade unions, large, resolutely anti-imperialist mass organizations, strongly opposed to all forms of imperialist world politics, appeared on the political stage. Many European statesmen were troubled by the question of whether the socialist parties and their millions of supporters would join in imperialist wars. When matters came to a head, however, the socialist's bark proved worse than his bite, and in 1914 national consciousness proved to be an overwhelming force even among the workers. The socialist administrations which later came to power in Britain and France were also forced to compromise on the colonial question.

Other elements in the anti-imperialist front were a number of associations with humanitarian and pacifist aims, such as the Liga für Menschenrechte (League for the Rights of Man) or the Protection of Aborigines Society (since 1837); exponents of peace movements and a league of nations; and literary and journalistic 'lone wolves' who pilloried cruelty and injustice, along the lines of Harriet Beecher Stowe (*Uncle Tom's Cabin*) and Eduard Douwes-Dekker (*Max Havelaar*), known under the pseudonym Multatuli. The tradition of philanthrophy had never been interrupted since the eighteenth century, and the achievements, the propaganda and practical steps taken by a Wilberforce in England and a Bishop Grégoire or a Victor Schoelcher in France were not forgotten. British propagandists saw to it that the Russian massacres among the Turkomans became known, and the Conservative outsider W. S. Blunt inveighed against British encroachments in Egypt and India. Emily Hobhouse was among those who protested against British treatment of Boer women and children, and Sir Roger Casement, among others, can claim credit for drawing the world's attention to atrocities in the Congo.

In Germany, there was no lack of indignation about excesses in the colonies. Berta von Suttner's book, *Die Waffen nieder* (Lay down your Arms), Alfred Nobel's famous foundation, and the books and exertions of Johann von Bloch in Russia may be cited as representative of the anti-war propaganda which was synonymous with anti-imperialist propaganda. It was in the nature of things that such militants often took a one-sided view of the situation, but their contribution to the cause of humanity undoubtedly remains their claim to fame. Parliamentary records provide an eloquent mine of information in this connection: from the interpellations of the bourgeois and socialist left wing in Germany to statements of opinion by the radicals in England, many examples indicate that a good many elected representatives pressed the moral aspect of imperialism and thereby indirectly ensured that its ethical components, far from being forgotten, became increasingly established. Already between 1880 and 1914, the principle of a pacifist-humanitarian internationalism, tending towards the League of Nations, was spreading throughout Europe, above nations and independent of political parties. This became a serious adversary of imperialism, even though the course of the Hague Conferences in 1899 and 1907 and, even more, the continuance of traditional international policies (which finally led to the First World War) showed where the real strength lay.

Finally, there were two other sources of resistance to imperialism which are less often discussed. First, there was that radical nationalism which did not wish to be distracted from its pursuit of European aims by experiments of a global, and particularly of a colonial, nature. The opposition of influential French politicians and their supporters to Ferry's imperialist programme was not least due to the desire for a concentration on the restoration of France's position of power in Europe and the recovery of Alsace-Lorraine.

Then there was the statesmanlike moderation, insight and scepticism which often enough put limits on over-ambitious imperialist plans. Even dyed-in-the-wool imperialists like Lord Salisbury or Count Witte made characteristically self-critical, doubtful or even monitory comments on the subject of imperialist politics. Many other European heads of government and foreign ministers give the impression that they conducted world politics in a subsidiary or even reluctant way, and that they would have preferred to restrict themselves to major European politics. Be that as it may, in the majority of imperialist world-political projects the responsible statesmen showed more caution than daring, more restraint than action.

IX IMPERIUM ET LIBERTAS

In his famous Guildhall speech in 1879 Disraeli said, 'When one of the greatest Romans was once asked what his politics consisted of he replied – *imperium et libertas*. That would not be a bad programme for a British Minister.' The classical quotation, which has not yet been identified, probably represents an unconscious adaptation by the British statesman of Tacitus' words *principatus et libertas*. The translation of an antique phrase into modern language nearly always involves a change in the meaning of the word, and Disraeli's presumably in-advertent revision of the Roman form underlines this fact. Be that as it may, the age of imperialism was furnished with a slogan and when the Primrose League was established in 1883, it chose *imperium et libertas* as its motto. By paraphrasing his programme in these terms, Disraeli had in mind merely an association between his country's old traditions of liberty and a resolute power policy in its foreign relationships. If we interpret Disraeli's *imperium* as imperialism and take *libertas* to be a profession of faith in modern democracy, a connection would in fact be established which does not entirely reveal the mystery of imperialism but makes its dialectic more com-prehensible.

It was only on the bases of freedom of association, freedom of assembly, freedom of the press and freedom of opinion that imperialism as a modern mass movement was possible. That is to say, only democracy made imperialism as we understand it possible; and even imperialism in the Tsarist autocracy, as later in the totalitarian states, could not dispense with a certain amount of modern democratic community life. Character-istically, arch-conservative and truly reactionary circles in many countries (though not all) wanted nothing to do with imperialism at first. The German gentry east of the Elbe (for example the Prussian Junkers) had reservations as a social class and a special interests group about the naval plans and overseas enterprises of the Reich's leadership. There were likewise Russian conservatives who would have nothing to do with pan-Slavism. Differences between the generations, however, must be taken into account. The conservative generation which had already grown up in the age of imperialism scarcely raised any further objections to expansionist power politics. In Britain it was the Diehards of right-wing Toryism who in the end provided the most energetic support for maintaining the Empire in the customary imperialist style. But this does not alter the fact that those who introduced and set themselves at the head of the imperialist movement came for the most part from the ranks of the progressives. Disraeli, an individualist who did not hunt with the pack and was anything but a typical Tory, cannot be used as a contradictory example. In France, many personalities of conservative tradition, such as Lyautey and Prince Henri d'Orléans, showed that the right was quick to endorse the idea of a Greater France, but it was the Liberal politician Ferry who actually made the breakthrough to colonial imperialism, and men such as the Secretary of State Eugène N. Etienne, the Minister of Colonial Affairs Gabriel Hanotaux, or the Radical Socialist politician Albert Sarraut

70 Benjamin Disraeli, the great and unconventional Prime Minister of mid-Victorian Britain as it entered the classical age of imperialism

71, 72 A view of the Amur river (1876) and a portrait of M. M. Muraviev, the great exponent of Russian expansion in the Far East

were pre-eminent in the consolidation of French imperialism. Russian history provides a liberal-imperialist prelude as early as the 1840s and 1850s: General Muraviev (later Muraviev-Amursky), appointed Governor-General of eastern Siberia by Nicholas I in 1847, followed a policy of Russian expansion in the Far East with the Tsar's concurrence. He hoisted the Russian flag at Fort Nikolayevsk at the mouth of the Amur in 1851; with the Treaty of Aigun he gained the Amur territory in 1858 from a China weakened by the Taiping Rebellion; and in 1860 he added the Ussuri area to this acquisition by the Treaty of Peking. Vladivostok was also founded in 1860.

These achievements assured the General a prominent place in the history of Russian imperialism. What concerns us here, however, is the opinions of this satrap which make him much different from the usual picture of a Russian nobleman devoted to Nicholas I. Bakunin said of Muraviev, who was nicknamed the 'red general' by St Petersburg society, 'He perceived Russia's greatness and glory in liberty.' Alexander Herzen characterized him more accurately as 'a democrat and a Tartar, a liberal and a despot'. Muraviev, who took an interest in the exiled Decembrists, was fascinated by the rise of the United States and its successful political principles. Like Herzen he had hopes that the United States would become Russia's future partner. Even if he himself did not do so, some of his officers dreamed of a free Siberia, to which they ascribed a liberal mission in Asia and Russia.

The liberal fireworks of Count Muraviev soon fizzled out, and a combination of Russian imperialism and liberalism which was sketched out during his period of office may in fact have become attached to his personality only by chance. But it was certainly no accident that leading pan-Slavists who later espoused the liberation of the serfs recognized that any effort by Russia as an *imperium* in foreign politics could succeed only if based on social and political reform. Many pan-Slavists pointed out in their writings that it was only through the reforms of the nineteenth century that Russia won a tenable international position. Only then had Russia been able to claim a moral right, in the sense of liberty and civilization, to strive for leadership among her Slav brothers. So-called Neo-Slavism (the enlightened form of pan-Slavism directed by Russia) was overwhelmingly in liberal hands during the last decade before the First World War.

In Britain's case, the fact remains that imperialism developed as a counter-movement to the liberalism of the doctrinaire Manchester school and to Little Englanderism. The forerunners, if not the fathers, of a policy of consolidating the British Empire were not, however, to the right of the Manchester group. These were the colonial reform radicals around Lord Durham and Gibbon Wakefield in the 1830s and 1840s who wanted to grant a large measure of self-determination to British overseas possessions, but, at the same time, supported colonization and wanted – without overtones of power politics – the world-wide unity of the Empire to be maintained. They converted quite a few personalities of the radical bourgeois left to their convictions. There are many reasons (though with reservations) to see in the work of this group a first step towards imperialism. The transition to imperialistic policy at the end of the nineteenth century also took place to some extent as a decision within the Liberal Party. W.E.Forster (founder and director of the Imperial Federation League), Prime Minister Lord Rosebery (leader of the Liberal Imperialists), Sir Charles Dilke, and finally Asquith, Grey and Haldane are examples of the many men in the Liberal camp who became pioneers of British imperialism; and it was from the ranks of radicalism that the great imperialist statesman, Joseph Chamberlain, came.

The combination of domestic and foreign political views in Dilke's famous early book, *Greater Britain*, seems characteristic of the *imperium et libertas* link, and bears out the thesis that the 'pan' movements fall within the scope of imperialism. Dilke's conception of a world community and – to all intents and purposes – a world dominated by the English-speaking peoples was based on the conviction of the inherent qualities of the Anglo-Saxon race, among which, of course, he counted of highest importance love of liberty and the faculty for democratic order in state and society. In a similar way, President Theodore Roosevelt sought the superiority of the Teutonic race in its democratic qualities. Throughout his public career, Dilke never made a secret of his decidedly democratic views regarding internal politics. Bonds of friendship connected him with Gambetta and other leaders of republican France. As a parliamentarian, he enjoyed the confidence of the young Labour Party. Yet this same man gave romantic reasons for holding on to the Indian possessions, occupied himself as a specialist with questions concerning the navy, army and general defence of the Empire, and unflaggingly pursued an imperialist line in foreign affairs. It would be wrong to interpret Dilke's attitudes and actions in domestic and foreign policy as contradictions, from which an outsider tried adventurously to create a synthesis.

73 A French cartoon of 1902 showing Theodore Roosevelt, astride Cuba and the Philippines, saying 'It is undeniable that the Anglo-Saxon race is at the head of civilization'

To many, indeed most, of Dilke's contemporaries, the simultaneous practice of imperialist world policies and a democratic domestic policy (including the white settlers' colonies) implied no contradiction. On the contrary, they were firmly convinced that one involved the other. The only question was the extent to which the non-white populations should be granted self-administration.

It is one of the characteristics of German political history that, on the whole, the democratic-imperialist connection never really came about as a conscious synthesis. Instead there was a widely held opinion that power politics in the foreign field corresponded to authoritarian domestic policies. This does not mean, of course, that there were no tendencies towards an

130 *imperium et libertas* programme. In addition to the moderate

Free Conservatives, the National Liberals above all stood out as imperialist supporters together with·men who had made their names in the Alldeutscher Verband. Many of them, such as Alfred Hugenberg or Heinrich Class, were by no means born conservatives. However, they saw their adversary less in agrarian reaction than in the liberalism of their fathers, which, for all its national consciousness, was still basically cosmopolitan and humanitarian. As the younger generation they went over to undiluted nationalism. Several individuals and groups of the German Freisinn, that is, left-wing liberal democrats, acknowledged imperialist aims. From these circles came Bernhard Dernburg, Secretary of State for the Colonies from 1907 to 1910 and later Vice-Chancellor, and Friedrich Naumann, formerly a Protestant parson, who founded the National-sozialer Verein (National-Social League), and was appointed first Chairman of the German Democratic Party in 1919. Naumann belonged to the most prominent advocates of imperialist-democratic policies in Germany. The great socio-logist Max Weber also ranks among the imperial democrats.

74 The character of Alberich in Wagner's *Nibelungen* operas, prime examples of German nationalism

The question of where in Germany the relationships of world politics abroad and democratic internal policies were most systematically and thoroughly treated is best answered by a reference to Naumann's writings. The Nationalsozialer Verein he founded at Erfurt in 1896 failed to attract the general public, but Naumann's influence on the young German intelligentsia of his time, both as publicist and orator, was all the more lasting. Shortly before his death, parliamentarians of the liberal left wing were able to exert considerable influence on the drafting of the Weimar Constitution. Naumann had originally placed his hopes in Wilhelm II, but he perceived later that this confidence in the 'Industrial and Naval Emperor' had been a delusion. Also his efforts to reconcile social democracy with the Empire, and to win over the power bloc of agrarian conservatives east of the Elbe in favour of imperialist democracy, had no success. But there is no doubt he recognized that the success of a great power in world politics depended ultimately on the combination of *imperium* and *libertas*. This explains his endeavours to catch up with the Western democracies' historical advantage and to correct reactionary defects of the German constitution. Naumann did a great deal to open the eyes of the younger generation of educated middle-class Germans to the social question. Thus a social component was added to the democratic elements of his imperialism.

X SOCIAL IMPERIALISM

'Democracy wants two things', said Austen Chamberlain: 'imperialism and social reform'. But does a tendency to social reform really join with imperialism or – to put it more broadly – does imperialism have its own social system? In trying to find an answer we must keep society as a whole in mind and not restrict ourselves to the 'social question', in the narrower sense of relations between employers and workers. The problem of the workers is, however, the central social problem of the age and must be our starting-point.

No imperialist, of course, wanted a revolutionary change in social relationships, but, unlike the preceding generation and many of their contemporaries, the imperialists realized that some kind of change was necessary. What has already been said about imperialist entrepreneurs applies to imperialists as a whole: there was a marked tendency towards social reform on the part of their political and intellectual leaders. In many cases imperialism and socialism (reformist, not Marxist) seemed to be different sides of the same coin. Indeed, almost all the foremost theoreticians of imperialism held that a progressive view in social affairs was the correlate of successful world politics. Stimuli came from various directions: from the social caesarism of Napoleon III and German social legislation; from Carlyle and the English Christian socialists. Social imperialism underwent a consistent development in both theory and practice particularly in Britain and Germany. There was, however, no question of a doctrine comparable to Marxism. The Liberal Imperialists associated with Lord Rosebery, Dilke, Asquith, Grey and Haldane were determined advocates of social reform. As champions of protective tariffs, Joseph Chamberlain and his supporters, including Halford Mackinder, political economist and geographer who was converted from Free Trade to

Protectionism, William Cunningham, theologian and economic historian, and W.J. Ashley, another political economist, emphasized the social progress to be expected from the abandonment of Free Trade. It was an active and distinguished minority that devoted itself to the triple aims of Protectionism, imperialism and social reform. An imperialist socialism was also advocated by individual leading members of the Fabian Society and fairly influential personalities without affiliations like the 'military socialist', Robert Blatchford. They too have to be mentioned here, though there is certainly a discrimination to be made between imperialists who conducted progressive social policies and social reform, and socialists who were also receptive to imperialist ideas.

In Germany, the democratic imperialists Max Weber and Friedrich Naumann supported social imperialism, and this was true also of the academic group known as the 'Kathedersozialisten' (professorial socialists), scholars and economic leaders who comprised the Verein für Sozialpolitik. It was not by chance that men like Gustav Schmoller, the economic historian who was Chairman of the Verein für Sozialpolitik for many years, the political economist Adolf Wagner, and many others, worked together with Max Weber and Friedrich Naumann to improve social conditions at the same time that they supported power politics; on the contrary, they established and energetically defended the mutual necessity of both.

The social element in the thinking of those Italian and German socialists who were won over (with appropriate reservations) to imperialist policies can be taken for granted. They too may be added to the broad and many-layered current of social imperialism. Marxist socialists and, for the most part, the British labour movement rejected social imperialism as a deception and a fraud; in many of their concepts they proved themselves a continuance of English radicalism, just as many of Hobson's radical views on imperialism flowed into the Marxist criticism of imperialism.

134

75 French magazine cover for May Day 1906, calling for an eight-hour workday ▶

l'assiette au beurre
Nº 265
28 Avril 19
50 centim
1er mai
8 HEURES DE TRAVAIL
8 HEURES DE SOMMEIL
8 HEURES DE LOISIR
Grandjouan

Imperialist Germany extended Bismarck's social legislation, and liberal-imperialist Britain likewise carried out a programme of social reform. In connection with individual social-political measures, such as the introduction of increasingly graded scales of social insurance, housing schemes, protective labour legislation, the beginning of shorter working hours, improved educational facilities and, particularly, the growing middle-class appreciation of the trade unions, more comprehensive social reform projects must be attributed to imperialism.

The reasoning of Cecil Rhodes sounds rather primitive today, although at the time it was defended even in scientific quarters and can be regarded almost as a *communis opinio* of imperialism. That great colonial pioneer summarized it as follows during a conversation with his friend W. T. Stead:

> Yesterday I attended a meeting of the unemployed in London and having listened to the wild speeches which were nothing more or less than a scream for bread I returned home convinced more than ever of the importance of imperialism . . . the great idea in my mind is the solution of the social problem. By this I mean that in order to save the forty million inhabitants of the United Kingdom from a murderous civil war the colonial politicians must open up new areas to absorb the excess population and create new markets for the products of the mines and factories. I have always maintained that the British Empire is a matter of bread and butter. If you wish to avoid civil war then you must become an imperialist.

Joseph Chamberlain's organization, the Tariff Reform League, put forward a programme according to which the Protectionist course would not only bring about economic prosperity and secure national unity, but also, at the core of social-political promises, would achieve full employment – a tempting prospect indeed in view of prevalent unemployment. The workers, however, would have had to carry the main burden of the indirect taxes proposed by the Protectionists, while Liberal

76 'The Strikers'; from a French journal, 1904

Imperialists continued their adherence to direct taxation in the most varied forms. Labour maintained the tradition of Free Trade radicalism and opposed the plans of Chamberlain and his supporters.

The social concept of imperialism, however, went even further than Rhodes's remarks to Stead or than the Protectionists' agitation would lead one to suppose. The national-minded middle class in the age of imperialism saw themselves faced with the basic fact of a class war that had become conscious and universally acknowledged. As for the workers, they went over to the Marxist camp in great numbers on the Continent. This was not the case in Britain where large groups of the working class continued to be represented by the Liberals even after the turn of the century. But there too the emergence of an independent workers' party signified a break in the community of political interests between employers and workers which had lasted for decades under the banner of radical

137

Liberalism. Confronted with this situation, it was Liberal Imperialism that sought an answer to the class war, a new possibility of national integration, since simple patriotism had obviously failed to fulfil this function for a considerable time. In this context many people proclaimed imperialism as the alternative to socialism. A good number believed, as E. Goulding put it, that 'the greatest obstacle that could be erected against the policy of the Labour Socialist Party was the policy of tariff reform linked with imperialism'. Imperialist answers to the class war differed in details according to their national and ideological origins; they could be liberal or anti-liberal, but the unifying and obligatory characteristics of all these efforts were the rejection of a revolutionary solution, maintenance of the existing form of society as far as ownership of the means of production was concerned, and devotion to one's own country. The imperialists as a whole countered the class-war formula with the idea of a national community with its national efficiency. It sometimes seemed as if foreign political activity and efforts towards imperial integration were being employed as a means to set national solidarity against class solidarity. In a related context, it was conjectured that the need to strengthen national consciousness was one of the reasons Bismarck turned to a colonial policy. Of course, imperialism frequently used power politics purely for the achievement of its own ends. But the subsidiary aim of establishing and consolidating the idea of a national community by such means was also pursued, and was openly acknowledged, by the most perceptive intellectuals of imperialism, such as the British-Canadian educationalist George Robert Parkin, one of the founders of the Imperial Federation League. Certain moral conquests in imperialism's favour were even gained in the party political camp of British, German and Italian socialism. A national socialism linked with imperialism began to take shape in several European countries long before the First World War. A special case in the extensive repertoire of this national social-ism was the portrayal of a nation in arms as the ideal community of life. In Germany, of course, there were many initiatives in this direction, but advocates of such thought patterns were by no means lacking elsewhere (for example Robert Blatchford in England). These protagonists not only drew their country-men's attention to the model of the German military organiza-tion, but also perceived in militarism the most expedient principle of social order if the nation was to be kept healthy and efficient. A further variant on the interdependence of social and national concepts was put forward by German and Italian publicists: the concept of transforming the class struggle into a national struggle, the view that the 'haves' and 'have-nots' of the world, proletarian and propertied nations, confronted each other. Such thoughts, of course, were entirely lacking in Great Britain, where the idea of organizing and elevating society so as to breed a truly imperial race became increasingly widespread. All these outlines had one common denominator: imperialism was trying to counter the class struggle with what Viscount Milner called 'a nobler socialism' and what international fas-cism was later to use with some success against international socialism – the idea of a national community.

Friedrich Naumann gave significant expression to the common denominator in the connection between imperialism and social reform. The manifesto of the Nationalsozialer Verein begins:

> We stand on nationalism in our belief that the unfolding of economic and political power by the German nation abroad is the prerequisite for all far-reaching social reforms at home. At the same time we are convinced that external power devoid of national consciousness cannot in the long run satisfy the politically interested masses. We therefore seek a power policy abroad and reform at home.

Many of Naumann's subsequent publications read like a simple paraphrase of this programme. In his *National Social Catechism* published in 1897, Naumann posed the question: 'How much does the spread of German influence around the globe depend on the national consciousness of the masses?' The answer: 'The tremendous sacrifices which must be made for the navy and the army if Germany is to mean anything in Asia, Africa, America and especially in Europe itself, cannot be imposed for long against the will of the working population.' Naumann expected a period of great wars caused by imperialist rivalry, and represented the view that Germany would be erased from history unless she took part. The question: 'Cannot the influence of all civilized peoples be spread in harmony?' was answered: 'No, because the market for these nations' goods is not large enough. This market grows more slowly than the urge of the civilized nations to expand. The struggle for the world market is a struggle for existence.'

Naumann could foresee success for Germany in world politics, but only if the German constitution were democratized and the working masses won over. He fought for the 'nationalizing of social democracy' and the setting up of a bloc from Bassermann to Bebel, that is, from the liberal right to the social democrats, excluding the conservatives and the ultramontanes. Conversely he felt that social progress could be guaranteed only if it was integrated into the nation's struggle for world power. 'Is there a good prospect for social reform in Germany? Yes, as soon as it is pursued in connection with the expansion of German power.' In 1900 Naumann summarized his views in a book called *Demokratie und Kaisertum* ('Democracy and Empire'). In it he again took up the view originated by Lorenz von Stein and Lassalle of a 'social royalty' and the close inner connection between the monarchy and the fourth estate. He applied this to the Hohenzollern Empire, whose imperialist character he attempted to delineate more closely by reference to the caesaristic, anti-reactionary and generally modern features of the system and, in particular, of Wilhelm II's personality. 'By raising the physical, mental and moral standards of the German worker', he wrote, 'the democratic movement is making a direct contribution to the German policy of expansion.'

XI IMPERIALISM AS REFLECTED IN LITERATURE AND ART

It is perhaps no accident that Britain alone produced an imperialist literature of distinction. As a pioneer of imperialism, Carlyle wrote historical and polemical works which rank as masterpieces of political prose. Charles Kingsley, who combined imperialist and Christian-socialist ideas, made a classical contribution to the historical novel with *Westward Ho!* in 1855, a didactic work with a nationalist purpose. This book was dedicated, among others, to Rajah Brooke, a typical example of the energetic white man overseas and therefore a man after the author's own heart. Kingsley was not the only one who revived the background of the Elizabethan age with the victory over the Spanish Armada as its climax, and sought to present an idealized picture of the past to serve as a model for his own times. Disraeli's novels, which occasionally betray his imperialist dreams, are interesting more because of the author's personality than their literary level. Imperialist novels which deserve mention are Sidney Dobell's *England's Day: A War Saga* (1871) and Geoffrey Drage's *Cyril* (1889).

The highest point of imperialist literature is probably represented by Rudyard Kipling's *Kim* (1901) or the wonderful short stories he wrote about the colonials in India. Kipling, who at forty-two was the first Englishman to receive the Nobel Prize for Literature, had many imitators at home and abroad, and inspired and edified leading British imperialist figures, such as Cecil Rhodes (who was said to have read only Kipling apart from the ancient classics), or men like the German colonial pioneer Carl Peters. There was no lack of imperialist novels of lesser calibre or even outright potboilers. Britain's imperial status and policies had a wide precipitation in lyrical and epic poetry. The most important of the Victorian generation were Tennyson ('Hands All Round', 1881; 'The Fleet', 1885; 'On the Jubilee of Queen Victoria', 1887) and Swinburne ('The Commonwealth', 'A Song for Unionists', 1886; 'The Armada', 1888). In 1884, Alfred Austin composed a poem on the occasion of the death of the imperialist politician, Sir Bartle Frere, and another on Dr Jameson's Raid in the Transvaal in 1896. Oscar Wilde adopted the imperialist note in his poem 'Ave Imperatrix' (1881), and Alfred Noyes tried to write a great imperialist national epic in *Drake, an English Epic* (1906–08). Cecil Rhodes was glorified not only by novelists but also by poets. Kipling may be allowed first place among imperialist poets as well as novelists. In any case, his verse tales, *Barrack Room Ballads*, belong in the history of literature. The title line of his poem, 'The White Man's Burden', intended for the Americans, became one of the slogans of European–American imperialism,

77, 78 Alfred Tennyson (below), Poet Laureate of imperialist Britain. His sequence of Arthurian poems, *Idylls of the King*, combined early British legends with a Christian mission. Left, Aubrey Beardsley's illustration of 'the achieving of the Sangreal'

and its theme was a justification for the world-wide intervention of the great powers. The self-confidence and self-awareness of imperialism found no other interpretation as telling as Kipling's.

Compared with the relevant English literature, the rich and creative writing of France is inferior in works of the imperialistic spirit. The ideas of Prévost-Paradol are reflected in the novels of Louis Bertrand, who lived in Algiers from 1891, and observed and described the 'new Latin race'. One aspect of the experience of imperialist existence – fulfilment in remote colonies, achievement, adventure, heroism, inner renewal, self-abnegating service to a worthwhile cause – may be perceived in one great French talent: Ernest Psichari, Renan's grandson. In dedicating his book *Terres de Soleil et de Sommeil* to Commandant Lenfant (who had himself written a book in 1905 entitled *La grande route de Tchad*), Psichari says:

> The happiest moments of life are perhaps those when one recalls past journeys and distant adventures. Since we left the ancient soil of Africa, I cannot stop visualizing the horizons we glimpsed during our eighteen months' stay in the land of the barbarians. . . . You, my Commandant, initiated me into a new life, the harsh and primitive life of Africa. You taught me to love that land of heroes, which you traversed unceasingly for nearly fifteen years. I am in debt to you for having given my life its reason and its purpose.

79, 80 Rudyard Kipling and Ernest Psichari, literary spokesmen for British and French imperialism

These lines express a feeling about life which is often encountered among imperialist idealists: the exalted consciousness of soldier and patriot. Yet the author's intention is remote from political propaganda. On the other hand, what was published as explicitly imperialist literature in France was often – though not always – forced, didactic, propagandistic, too deliberate, and the most extreme opposite of art for art's sake. We are not concerned with the sort of exoticism which produced noteworthy works in France; nor with psychological novels on colonial and native themes. We are concerned only with authors whose aim was to produce sentiments consonant with 'l'Empire Français'; among these, Pierre Mille, an admirer and imitator of Kipling's, deserves first mention. Mille was London correspondent in the Madagascar General Secretariat in 1895. He praised the vigour of Leopold II in his travel-diary *Au Congo Belge* (1899) and viewed Africa as the energy-reservoir of France too. In many of his later works he took up such questions as the preservation of a humanitarian attitude outside the European world, the relationship between Europeans and natives, race, miscegenation and the threat to the white race. At the centre of Mille's stories is the colonial soldier Barnavaux, an imitation of the type created by Kipling in *Soldiers Three*: the unknown soldier of the colonial army, the simple man serving an imperialist policy. And Pierre Mille makes this policy a service for the regeneration and glorious future of the French nation, but also understood as a service for all of white Europe. Since on the whole the climax of French colonial imperialism was not reached until after the First World War, it was not until 1921 that a Grand Prix de Littérature Coloniale was founded. In 1928, Pierre Mille became the head of a newly formed Société des Ecrivains et Romanciers Coloniaux. The distribution of literary prizes (there was also a special prize for France's Indo-Chinese possessions) was based much more on considerations of content than aesthetic quality.

There was one aspect of French colonial-imperialist journalism and literature which was totally foreign to Britain. This was the effort to overcome the 'Latin' inferiority complex, which had grown particularly as a result of the defeat in 1870–71, but which goes back to other causes and has a parallel in the anxieties and activities of some of the Spanish 'Generation of 1898'. The assertion that the Romanic nations were decadent was not only widespread in English and German literature, but was also echoed and believed by the French themselves. Quite a number of serious and intelligent men exerted themselves, on the basis of this supposed fact, to discover a way to recovery, and many saw a powerful imperialist policy as the right means.

Imperialism is scantily reflected in Russian and German literature, even though this was a time when neither lacked outstanding talents. Soloviev's stories of the Antichrist and his poems are concerned with 'the yellow peril' – the representation of global struggles, as they fit into the ideological arsenal of imperialism. Gustav Frenssen, a German author who was much read but certainly not exceptional, wrote a book called *Peter Moors Fahrt nach Südwest* ('Peter Moor's Odyssey'), in which a young artisan from Holstein gives an account of the campaign against the Hereros. Hans Grimm, a significant writer of colonial tales and author of the influential novel *Volk ohne Raum* (1928), attained prominence only after the First World War. 'Volk ohne Raum' certainly made history as a slogan. In Grimm's work there was a peculiar polarity between his overseas commitment and his devotion to his native soil and heath, that is, between the colonial novel and the type which is termed 'Heimatkunst' in German literary history. The connection between these two elements is probably not arbitrary, but is based on a common denominator. In both cases the aim was the moral and physical well-being of the German people, the presumed truth and reality, what was useful to the whole nation. The fact that, in both cases, these efforts were only rarely convincingly successful, already gave Grimm's contemporaries food for thought.

It was hardly surprising that British imperialist literature had the advantage over all other relevant countries. But it would be an exaggeration to say that an imperial consciousness had taken shape and been diffused only in Britain. The supporters of imperialism were everywhere a minority, but the phenomenon itself was so fascinating that one wonders why more writers on the Continent were not drawn by its spell. It is not that most of the authors to be taken into consideration were at that time leftists. One reason may be that many potentially imperialist writers on the Continent, such as Barrès, Bainville, Maurras, were still too occupied with national (and that means not yet imperialist) themes. On the other hand, the didactic patriotic literature, formerly so cultivated, had already deteriorated artistically by the turn of the century. It is noticeable that the theme of so-called imperialist literature is overwhelmingly colonialism. Perhaps the very colourfulness of the subject, which stimulated the writer's imagination, is sufficient explanation of the preference for colonial subjects. In reverse, apart from anti-colonial writers, or more strictly writers critical of colonialism, such as Multatuli, Farrère, Maupassant and Fabre, there was scarcely an anti-imperialist literature worthy of the name.

81 Monument of Commandant Marchand, facing the Musée de la France d'Outre Mer, Paris (*see* Ill. 91)

82, 83, 84 The Albert
Memorial, London, and the
accompanying motifs
representing Europe (left
above) and Africa (left)

Imperialism had an even smaller effect on the plastic arts than on literature. In any case, the synchronization of artistic epochs with political periods occurs only in exceptional cases. But many of the powerful political trends do project themselves into the sphere of literature and art, and are echoed there. The close link between nationalism and imperialism is shown, among other things, by the fact that both documented their desire for historical perpetuation and the creation of a mass consciousness of history by setting up commemorative tablets, statues, monumental architecture and memorial halls, which

147

seem rather questionable to us today. The strong yearning to historicize an epoch is expressed not only in the convictions of those who commissioned these works, but also in their execution. If one compares the Vittorio Emanuele Monument in Rome, as a typical example of a national memorial, with the memorial to Cecil Rhodes in Cape Town, there are no great differences in their conception. The plan of the Rhodes sepulchre in the Matabele Mountains is another matter; this may more easily be called a successful attempt to create a proper imperial style. The Bismarck Monument in the port of Hamburg reveals its creator's wish to raise the small German national state to imperialism, not only in the choice of location but also in its form. Attempts were made all over the world before and after 1914 to do justice artistically to imperialist achievements in a series of memorials which owed little to tradition.

87 'Here lie the remains of Cecil John Rhodes': the sepulchre in the Matabele Mountains

88 The grandiose memorial to Rhodes in Cape Town

85, 86 Different styles in monumental imperialist art. Far left, the monument in Khartoum to General Gordon, hero of British military colonialism; left, the Bismarck Monument in Hamburg (*cf.* p. 68)

89, 90 British architecture in India.
Right, buildings by Sir Edwin Lutyens
in New Delhi. Below, the
Victoria Memorial in Calcutta

Half-baked historicized imitations of European architecture
were recklessly transmitted overseas; as a rule, one can scarcely
speak of art in these cases. In areas like Siberia, which had never
developed their own advanced culture, when the national
Russian style (for example, in church architecture) was trans-
planted and carried on, this caused no disturbance – especially
as there was no contrast to the landscape. It was all the more
distressing when the worst European clichés were spread out
against the background of Asia's highly cultivated memorial

architecture; moreover, most of them were totally un-suited to the peculiarities of the landscape. Imperialism must be given credit, on the other hand, for making the first praise-worthy and successful efforts to care for and preserve splendid memorials of indigenous architecture abroad. Lord Curzon and Marshal Lyautey deserve special mention in this regard. Attempts by European architects to adapt their work in the colonies to indigenous forms deserve interest; indeed, they sometimes translated (as in the Musée de la France d'Outre Mer in Paris) motifs from overseas, with full consciousness of their imperialist purpose.

The buildings of the Indian Parliament and the Governor-General's Palace (now the residence of the President of the Republic of India) in New Delhi are a rather interesting achieve-ment of European sympathy with a foreign culture and at the same time a witness of modern imperialist thought. The architect, Sir Edwin Lutyens, had built masterpieces in his homeland which were bound to their settings and deeply traditional – an example, as in the case of Hans Grimm, of the inner polarity between 'Heimatkunst' and imperialist trends. The effect is disconcerting, however, when a British architect transplants a Far Eastern building style to Africa, as in the case of the University of Legon near Accra. The universalism of empire and commonwealth might have contained the temptation of a syncretic style; but modern art, and particularly the plastic arts, pursued syncretism of style only occasionally. That 'international style', now stamped on all the cities of the world, has won. And when we examine architecture and the other plastic arts for what they can reveal about spiritual but also political phenomena, they tell us unequivocally that the future no longer belongs to imperialism, but to a new internationalism, which has yet to be filled with content.

91 Façade of the Musée de la France d'Outre Mer, also called the Musée des Colonies

XII IMPERIALISM AND LEARNING

The exploitation of the natural sciences by imperialist politics is obvious; the advancement of these branches of learning and research by state and private enterprise was inevitably dictated, independently of imperialism, by the necessities of industrial society. The gap which had opened between advancing scientific and technological knowledge and social conditions could best be filled by the spread of more 'useful' knowledge. The explicit or implicit tendency towards the welfare state and the affluent society depended absolutely on a more comprehensive integration of natural scientific knowledge. The requirements of the period, in their turn, reacted upon research in the natural sciences and technology in such a way that problems posed by industry, the military and transport exercised a special attraction; private and public funds granted financial support more generously in these fields than elsewhere; and the organization of scientific endeavour itself was transformed to meet the exigencies of the age.

Yet the autonomous sphere of research continued to exist, in which, relatively independent of contemporary needs and hopes of profit, and driven by the urge to investigate and professional curiosity, one could venture into 'pure' science – altruistic and without regard for any practical gain. Such a nucleus of pure scholarship existed (and still exists) in the humanities, which, on the basis of traditional education, were considered by the public in the imperialist age to be more distinguished than the natural sciences. Despite the structural difference of these disciplines and protestations of disinterest, experts in the humanities were also stimulated and influenced in no small measure by their times. This should not be thought of as a criticism, but rather as an affirmation of the fact that the humanities, by their very nature, have an intimate connection with the vagaries of politics and society, and with the changes in historical perspectives that correspond to them. It might have been opportunism if a philospher, a historian or a representative in related fields tried *as a scholar* to conform to the age of imperialism and put himself forward as its spokesman. But as a rule it was something more and something very different: namely, the need of the scholar educated in the humanities knowingly to sink himself and fit into his own period, and to interpret it correctly. Moreover, there was the idea that learning too must be placed at the service of the nation; thus the theoretician could provide solutions which, in their end effect, were eminently practical.

The stimuli which the age procured for learning were balanced by those which emanated from learning. The sciences did not only receive, they gave as well and they grasped initiatives which – popularized and vulgarized – had a definite effect on the thoughts and actions of contemporaries. Very often the priority lay with the sciences.

PHILOSOPHY

Three philosophical movements above all gained contact with imperialist thought and helped to form its ideologies. First, Oxford 'Neo-idealism', led by scholars like Thomas Hill Green, Herbert Bradley and Bernard Bosanquet in Oxford itself, but also represented outside Oxford by notable figures, such as the Scottish university lecturers, Edward Caird and William Wallace. Whereas Carlyle's irrationalism and somewhat crude handling of the relationship between power and justice had made no great impression on the British public, these professional scholars developed a system on a higher level that did not fail to attract the British intelligentsia. The main themes of this school of thought (which interests us here less for its philosophical distinction than for its relationship with imperialism) may be identified as the historical determinism of the universe, and not least of the state and justice; the concept of the historical-social universe as an organism; the primacy of man's ethical nature, his strength of will and his moral motivation; the existence of a metaphysical unity. The historical-philosophic constructions of this school give the conception of Empire – primarily the British Empire, of course – an elevated status, indeed the highest place among all manifestations of social organization. In his book *The Nation's Awakening* (1896), Spenser Wilkinson, a pupil of the Oxford Neo-idealists, expressed very clearly what certain British imperialists hoped for in their philosophy:

> If the British Empire is to fill its true place in the world it must first find its true place in the heart of its own subjects: they must have a reason for the national faith that is in them. That reason will be given by the analysis of the laws of British power and of the conditions which justify its exercise. This final inquiry will set out not from the assumption that might is right, which is the creed of despotism and the argument of caprice, nor from the theory that right is might, which is the mistake of shallow enthusiasts, but from the conviction that the universe is the manifestation of an intelligible order, inseparable from the order revealed in the processes of thought; that the laws of the material and of the moral world arise from the same sources, and are but different aspects of the same reality.

Balliol and New College in Oxford ranked as the main bastions of Neo-idealism. Oxford students stamped with the spirit of Neo-idealism included the 'proconsul' Alfred Milner, Arnold Toynbee (senior and junior), and Liberal Imperialists like Asquith and Grey. Haldane was a student of the Neo-idealist Caird in Glasgow and of the German Idealist Lotze in Göttingen; he was also active as a philosopher himself. Milner gathered round him in South Africa a group of young men from Balliol and New College, who became known as 'Milner's Kindergarten' and proved to be outstanding representatives of

British imperialism's late phase: Leopold S. Amery, Lionel Curtis, Patrick Duncan and Philip Kerr (later Lord Lothian).

The original classical German Idealism had already had its effect on Carlyle and Wordsworth, and the opponents of British Neo-idealism characterized this disapprovingly as a German product:

> The Rhine has flowed into the Thames, at any rate into those upper reaches of the Thames, known locally as the Isis, and from the Isis the stream of German idealism has been diffused over the academical world of Great Britain. It would be natural to look to an idealistic philosophy for a counterpoise to those crude doctrines of physical force which we shall find associated with the philosophy of science. Yet, in the main, the idealistic movement has swelled the current of retrogression. It is itself, in fact, one expression of the general reaction against the plain, human, rationalistic way of looking at life and its problems. Every institution and every belief is for it alike a manifestation of a spiritual principle, and thus for everything there is an inner and more spiritual interpretation. Hence, vulgar and stupid beliefs can be held with a refined and enlightened meaning, known only to him who so holds them. [L. T. Hobhouse, *Democracy and Reaction*]

Neo-idealism in Germany itself found its only representation, in any way comparable to the British school, in the much-read, influential and clever popularizer Rudolf Eucken, a Nobel Prize winner; while some representatives of New Kantianism approached Revisionist Socialism. This juxtaposition must be qualified, however, by the fact that old-fashioned Idealism continued to be taught as a 'religion' in German schools at a time when it had receded well into the background in university lecture halls. Neo-idealism should certainly not be overestimated as a school of thought in the history of philosophy. But its importance was considerable as an intellectual signpost and a lead for the political rulers of British imperialism, as well as for the followers of German imperialism, consisting mainly of the educated middle class – for example, the disciples of the historian Ranke, known as the 'Ranke Renaissance' group.

The philosophical counterpart to Idealism and Neo-idealism, during the age of imperialism and even before, was Positivism, which was firmly based on the natural sciences. None the less, it also offered numerous arguments for imperialism in all the great European nations – mainly in the form of Social Darwinism. Among the representatives of biologism, Social Darwinism and racialism – who did not incidentally constitute a closed group but developed the most varying views – there were many who were not professional philosophers but who had made a name for themselves as doctors, eugenicists, sociologists, ethnographers, biologists, anthropologists, and in other branches of natural science. These men, who tried to achieve a philosophical synthesis from their empirical starting-point, included such figures as the 'biometrician' Karl Pearson who envisaged cultural progress for mankind as a mutual struggle of extermination between the stronger peoples or races; the sociologist F. H. Giddings; anthropologists like Ernst Haeckel, Ludwig Woltmann and Count Vacher de Lapouge. They were joined by men like the high-ranking officer Gustav Ratzenhofer; Benjamin Kidd, civil servant and later political journalist; the jurist and political economist Ludwig Gumplowicz. Finally, distinguished dilettantes like the French philosophical writer Count Arthur Gobineau, and Houston St Chamberlain, the Englishman turned German, should be mentioned. An incomplete manuscript on Darwinism by the pan-Slav author, Danilevsky, is said to exist.

The doctrinal differences within biological Positivism and the conclusions drawn from them were extraordinarily great. The applicability of the doctrines of the struggle for existence and natural selection to the survival of the fittest in imperialist politics is self-explanatory. It seems remarkable that many advocates of racial Positivism sought to link the struggle between nations in the province of external affairs and world politics with the realization of democratic ideals at home, and regarded it as the task of democracy to create the best conditions for the survival of their own country in the competitive struggle among peoples or even to prepare the way for a race of 'supermen', as Giddings put it. Kidd, for instance, in opposition to individualism and socialism, sought to limit the 'internal' Social Darwinism of class conflict, in order to strengthen the nation for the 'external' Social Darwinism of the struggle between races and nations. Other scholars of the Social Darwinist stamp inclined towards a romantic aristocracy as a social and political ideal at home as well as abroad and emphasized the point of view of a master race within the social world. The anti-imperialist L. T. Hobhouse believed Neo-idealism and Social Darwinism to be two variants of one reactionary opposition to genuine progress, namely the humanitarian and utilitarian path to an ethical internationalism.

Nowadays, along with Neo-idealism and Social Darwinist Positivism, *Lebensphilosophie* (a philosophy based on human experience) is regarded as another current which is peculiar to imperialism. In *Die Zerstörung der Vernunft* ('The Destruction of Reason'), a book in which the history of German thought is analyzed from the Marxist viewpoint, George Lukács introduces Friedrich Nietzsche as the founder of 'irrationalist imperialism' and Wilhelm Dilthey as the founder of imperialist *Lebensphilosophie*. These are followed by Oswald Spengler and Max Scheler, and finally by a series of individuals described as prefascist or fascist advocates of *Lebensphilosophie*. In conformity with his doctrine, Lukács had to claim a universal validity for the combination of imperialism and *Lebensphilosophie*. And yet, apart from certain literary testimonials, there are no learned works on *Lebensphilosophie* worth mentioning in Great Britain, the classical land of imperialism, not to speak of Russia. *Lebensphilosophie* was restricted to Germany and France, and possibly related features may be discovered in Italy. Even if Lukács's way of identifying imperialism with *Lebensphilosophie* remains contrived, it must still be admitted that a generation which valued the love of deeds and action above all could feel con-

92 Friedrich Nietzsche (1844–1900), the German philosopher whose views were appropriated by imperialist thinking

firmed by *Lebensphilosophie*, and that imperialist intellectuals were glad to appeal to a doctrine which put instinct against reason, myth against system, and the (supposedly) healthy against the (allegedly) ill. Through careful examination of literary and journalistic evidence, through biographical and sociological studies, and also through a survey of the academic philosophical tendencies, one can obtain an idea of the influence of a theory on the educated public, as well as those masses who are reached more or less only by slogans and simplifications. On this basis a sizable proportion of the imperialist mentality may be attributed to *Lebensphilosophie* and its related doctrines. Nietzsche was certainly one of the gods secretly or openly worshipped by many imperialists. At the same time it is remarkable that, in general, only the extreme reactionary wing of imperialism and later of fascism laid claim to *Lebensphilosophie*; democratic imperialism as a whole rested on other philosophical grounds.

HISTORY

Imperialism embraced history even more intimately than it did philosophy. This applies to countless works of empirical historiography, as well as to the historical ingredients in journalism, attempts at historical interpretation and, lastly, to several concepts of a philosophy of history. To account for this, we should take into consideration the fact that history, by its very nature, is very close to politics; that there is a need to bestow on contemporary events some kind of meaning and to bolster it with historical justification; and that history is in its own right a political and actively instructive branch of learning. At any rate the fact remains that contemporary trends of history and imperialism promoted and benefited each other. We find champions of imperialism both among historians of the old, more rhetorical and narrative school, and among those with a more modern, methodical training in philology and critical evaluation. Many of them distinguished themselves as party politicians, parliamentarians, editors of journals, and as members of, and spokesmen for, imperialist propaganda organizations; but we are concerned here only with the imperialist slant in these political professors' learned works or in those by like-minded amateurs. Mikhail P. Pogodin, head of the older school of Russian pan-Slavism, was a professional historian who combined the promotion of Slavic studies with political propaganda. N. Y. Danilevsky's *Russia and Europe*, the chief work of pan-Slavism, originated from the pen of a scientist but was presented by its author mainly in the form of a historical-psychological and a historical-philosophical 'investigation into the cultural and political relationships of the Slav and Germano-Romanic worlds'. Of the imperialist historians in Great Britain, John R. Seeley attracted the most attention – outside Britain too, especially in France and Germany; his book *The Expansion of England* caused a sensation. J. A. Cramb, Professor of Modern History at Queen's College, London, and a member of the Oxford Neo-idealist group, found less response abroad. In his main work, *The Origin and Destiny of Imperial Britain*, he gave a historical-philosophical interpretation of the imperial concept. Cramb regarded the imperialist organization of the state as the highest and most perfect after the stages of city-state, feudal state, class state, and national democratic state had become obsolete. The British Empire, in contrast to the old Holy Roman Empire, the Papacy, Venice, Spain and France, was the crowning achievement of the Teutonic race and a culmination in world history complying with the ideals of freedom and tolerance issuing from the Reformation. This conclusion, he held, contained within itself all previous phases of history and 'elevated' them.

France too did not lack imperialist historians: Gabriel Hanotaux, professor and Minister for the Colonies, is a perfect representative of the type, though it must be added at once that, in terms of his theme, he remained a peripheral figure among his tribe. The line of study followed by the overwhelming majority of French historians was not dictated by the imperialist current of the time. German historians, too, even if they gave full support to Wilhelmine imperialism, considered the national history of the fatherland to be their primary task. They were so immersed in the emergence of Little German unity that they had little time left for writing imperialist history in a grand style. Yet there were a number of gifted historians in the so-called Ranke Renaissance group, including Dietrich Schäfer, Erich Marcks, Max Lenz and Hans Delbrück, who spent a considerable amount of their energy on imperialist subjects, who attempted to graft Ranke's doctrine of the European state system on to world politics, and who sought a synthesis between their professional activities and their patriotic efforts on behalf of Germany's world position. The most successful German historical work on imperialism, however, *Weltgeschichte in Umrissen* ('World History in Outline'), was written not by one of the professional experts but by an outsider, Colonel Graf Maximilian Yorck von Wartenburg. Oswald Spengler's study in the philosophy of history, *The Decline of the West*, did not appear until after the First World War but had been conceived prior to that event. For all its general pessimism, this book can be construed and was intended as an imperialist work.

GEOGRAPHY

The political involvement which led historians towards the path of imperialism achieved the same effect among geographers. The geographical societies in European capitals, as already mentioned, were straightforward laboratories of imperialism. Geographers travelling for research purposes were often given political missions and their political interests were stimulated through contact with colonial administrations. At all events geographers were considered to be of much greater value than historians as experts in matters of world politics, and in this context we can associate with them China, India, Africa and related specialists. Every European great power included explorers among its advisers, agents or political activists during the age of imperialism. The complete spectrum of imperialist convictions can be found even among those geographers whose

93, 94, 95 Three works by the German artist, Emil Nolde, showing the interest in foreign places and people which was one of the results of imperialism. Left, Japanese woman with musical instrument; left below, three Siberians; below, South Seas native

96, 97 The H. M. Stanley medal of the Royal Geographic Society (1889), commemorating the Emin Pasha Relief Expedition

countries did not or could not pursue world power claims. From this point of view, a clear distinction cannot be made, for instance, between Sven Hedin's learned publications and his political writings.

In 1897 the German geographer, Friedrich Ratzel, published his *Politische Geographie*, in which he dealt with the natural conditions of politics, and analyzed the relationship between state and space. As anthropology from the one side pressed forward as a political science, so Ratzel's work gave impetus to geopolitics, a discipline which, by its nature, was intended as an applied science, and which exerted some influence on the political ideas of imperialism. John Halford Mackinder of England, Rudolf Kjellén of Sweden and Karl Haushofer of Germany were the most important exponents of geopolitics. Mackinder, whose writings include *The Geographical Pivot of History* (1904) and *Britain and the British Seas* (1902), was the father of the 'heartland theory' and considered himself a political educator of his country. A political professor, he extended his activities simultaneously to scholarship, political journalism and party politics. Director of the London School of Economics from 1903 to 1908, Mackinder was an adherent of the group of Liberal Imperialists under Lord Rosebery and was one of the theoreticians of imperialism. Later, converted to Chamberlain's plans for protective tariffs, he went over to the Unionists. On several occasions he was given political responsibility, and yet he never became a key figure in the political world nor did his doctrines have a very wide effect. By its nature the doctrine of geopolitics could appeal only to intellectual minorities, and it was on the part of such groups that Mackinder found attention and agreement in England and, not least, in the United States during the Second World War.

In the combination of scholarship and politics Mackinder symbolized the effort of geopolitics to become political practice. This was true also of Professor Rudolf Kjellén, author of *Great Powers* (1905) and *The State as Life-Form* (1917), who, in contrast to Mackinder, started out from the premise that the state was an actual and individual organism. Kjellén belonged to the reformist wing of the Swedish Conservative Party and, like Mackinder, was an active parliamentarian without any notable political successes to record. As a prominent member of the pro-German 'Activists', he advocated support for the Central Powers in the First World War and was appointed by the King to a secret parliamentary committee which advised the monarch on questions of foreign policy. Kjellén continued to sympathize with the German cause after the war and, as was only to be expected, found a great response in Germany. This had its effect on the acceptance of his theory of the state. The German school of geopolitics strove, along Kjellén's lines, to conceive of the state not only as a legal entity but also as a biological quantity, a natural, living organism that had to fight for its existence. Professor (and General) Karl Haushofer, who edited a later edition of Kjellén's *Great Powers*, was head of the German geopoliticians and personified the typical imperialist scholar who taught and was active in the fields of politics and learning. Yet he did not make his mark until after the age of imperialism.

XIII IMPERIALIST WELTANSCHAUUNG AND ATTITUDES TO LIFE

98
British colonials:
polo in India

What we have said about imperialism in general applies also to its *Weltanschauung*: it was not to everybody's taste, nor can it be used to define the epoch. We can establish a distinct ideological need only among minorities, while the rest – in so far as they were inclined at all towards a spiritual explanation of their time – were satisfied with an iron ration of moral admonitions or with the general experience of life and practical wisdom.

We must try to reach behind the façade of official and officious ideologies and ascertain what basic spiritual attitudes motivated those people who subscribed to imperialism and on what their *Weltanschauung* was founded. Moreover, it must be noted that there can be no question of a uniform conviction and a uniform attitude to life. Just as the imperialist could be influenced philosophically by Idealism but also by scientific Positivism; just as he could be committed politically to an aristocratic or a democratic concept; just as one could fight against utilitarianism while others understood how to gain huge profits through imperialist policies – so the imperialist's psychological constitution revealed an extraordinarily wide range. Many elements in the imperialist *Weltanschauung* have a markedly dialectical relationship with one another.

ETHOS OF SERVICE AND CULT OF POWER

These are both characteristically linked together in imperialism. Imperialists with high ethical standards always regarded themselves as serving a great cause: the defence of their country, coupled with its honour and glory; the fulfilment of humanitarian aims; and the achievement of an equitable world order.

165

It cannot be denied that very many people took these things seriously and that they confirmed this by their willingness to face death on the battlefield or expose their life and health to the gravest risks through daring activities in murderous climates or in unusual and threatening circumstances. The deeds of scientific investigators and explorers, the struggle against slavery, the patient dedication of so many government servants and doctors to their tasks, and the devotion to duty of numerous officers and soldiers represent concrete arguments against any attempt to bring 'devotion to duty' into doubt as an empty phrase. The best example of the literary glorification of the virtues of service is Carlyle, whose writings express a spirit of opposition to the commercialism of his times and especially Manchesterism. In place of calculation and considerations of utility, he and other authors of similar views represented the idea of doing things not because of profit but for their own sake, and the valuation of action from moral and social viewpoints. If Carlyle, in the style of a nineteenth-century hellfire preacher, distinguished between good and bad epochs, he did attribute to the former faith, charity, social peace and, above all else, altruism – altruism, however, not as an excess of emotion, but as social behaviour. Carlyle's high esteem for, and emphasis on, work, which he regarded as a moral obligation rather than a commodity, were among his modern characteristics opposed by a good many reactionaries. The idealization and adulation of work and professional achievement were capable of exerting strong impulses in the world of gigantic industrial organization and bureaucratic systems, and without doubt they did so. The number of people who devoted themselves almost exclusively to their work and drew their self-confidence from it manifestly continued to grow in the course of the nineteenth and twentieth centuries. The qualities which Carlyle praised and wished to propagate were valued in Germany as 'Prussian virtues'. Their applicability to the conditions of the nineteenth and twentieth centuries, and especially to imperialist politics, is beyond question. Lyautey's publications, and not least the essay already mentioned, *Du Rôle social de l'officier*, contain extremely impressive examples of a service mentality. Lord Curzon's works also fall into this category: his book, *British Government in India* (1925), although couched in a histrionic language now strange to us and in ardent pursuit of imperialist aims, tried to deflate cheap enthusiasm and lift the veil from the concealed *via dolorosa* of Britons in India, from the simplest private to the Viceroy himself. He quoted Thackeray's Colonel Newcombe:

> What a strange pathos seems to me to accompany all our Indian story! Besides that official history which fills Gazettes and embroiders banners with the name of victory, which gives moralists and enemies cause to cry out at English rapine, and smaller patriots to boast of invincible British valour – besides the splendour and conquest, the wealth and glory, the crowned ambition, the conquered danger, the vast prize, and the blood freely shed in winning it – should not one remember the tears too? Besides the lives of myriads of British men, conquering on a hundred fields from Plassey to Myanee, and bathing them *cruore nostro*, think of the women and the tribute which they perforce must pay to those victorious achievements.

And in another passage he cites extracts from a letter by Lord Dalhousie: 'But seven years' heavy experience enables me to declare that emoluments, honours and reputation are as a feather against what must be set in the other balance in India.' Curzon finishes with the words:

> True it is that the tribute has had to be paid for nearly two centuries, not by Governors General and Viceroys alone, but by English men and English women of every class of life and service in India. But I have sought to show here that even the most highly placed cannot escape, and that over the Viceregal throne there hangs not only a canopy of broidered gold but a mist of human tears. I think that the majority of those who have suffered have done so without repining; they have thought the price worth paying; perhaps even they

would do it again. But at least let their countrymen know that they pay it, and remember that the foundation stones of the Indian Empire which they vaunt so loudly have not merely been laid in pride and glory, but have been cemented with the heart's blood of stricken men and women. And equally would I say to the Ministers who sit in state in Downing Street and the officials who rule and overrule from Whitehall, and to the legislators at Westminster who are often so ready with criticism and so glib with censure – that they may derive some profitable lessons from the history of the past, and may learn that the government of India is not a pastime but an ordeal, not a pageant alone but as often a pain. As for the Governor-General or the Viceroy who has laboured there, peradventure as he leaves those shores for the last time he may find solace in the words of Edmund Burke: 'If I were to call for a reward it would be for the services in which for fourteen years without intermission I showed the most industry and had the least success. I mean the affairs of India. They are those on which I value myself the most: most for the importance; most for the labour; most for the judgement; most for constancy and perseverance in the pursuit.'

Carlyle, like his kindred spirits in Germany during the age of imperialism, Lyautey like Curzon, had no doubt that only he who disposed of power could succeed in serving a noble cause. This exercise of power could be understood as a temporary and indispensable period on the way towards an exalted aim or as an expression of the eternal law that the stronger must dominate the weaker and the superior the more humble – and indeed for the benefit and welfare of those being governed. Power could be a means to an end, but it could also be conceived as an end in itself. The distinction we have made here in theory was less often true in practice. The idea of service was in reality largely tied up with the possession of power, and the imperialists would not have been human if they had not sought compensa-

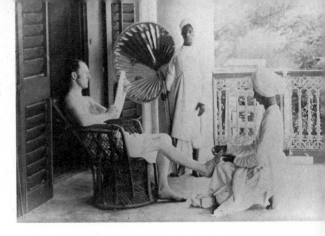

99 The British officer in
India, c. 1870

tion for the rigours of their service in the cruder or more
sublime enjoyment of power. The fascination and ennoblement
of power were in any case stock aspects of imperialist behaviour.
The imperialist type, whose training became a matter of concern
for so many leading spirits of the age, had authoritarian traits; he
had to feel certain of his superiority and assert it with emphasis.
Imperialism was basically power politics. While warlike efforts
were not absolutely necessary for political success, there was
no lack of admiration when that did occur. The founding of the
German Reich in 1871 and the personality of Bismarck
strengthened the 'power policy' mentality in both Great
Britain and Russia, and thus influenced directly or indirectly
the transition of those states to imperialism. Many German
intellectuals viewed world politics as the inevitable consequence
of the advent of the powerful national state. Thus spoke the
sociologist Max Weber in 1895 on the occasion of his inaugural
lecture:

> We must grasp the fact that the unification of Germany was
> a youthful prank played by the nation in her old age, and
> which she would have been well advised to forgo because
> of the cost if it turns out to be the conclusion and not the
> starting-point of a German policy of world power. . . . We
> will not succeed in lifting the curse under which we stand –
> a generation born after a stirring political epoch – unless we
> learn to be something different: precursors of a greater age.

169

Imperialism was far removed from the radicalism of movements that conceived of themselves as the heralds of a new age in world history, whose victory would usher in a new chronology. It inclined rather to the influential contemporary current of historical thinking and felt the power of continuity particularly in national history. Imperialist historians and pamphleteers tried to derive from the past the mission of universal scope to be fulfilled by their countries and sought to find inspiration for the present from great historical examples. It scarcely needs to be said that the interpretations of history were often extremely modish and sometimes even downright arbitrary; in short, they were historical ideologies. Imperialism is certainly no exception in this respect. Awareness of history has hitherto almost always required the detour of historical ideology to attain widespread effect. But the number of professional and amateur historians among imperialist theoreticians is nevertheless striking. The imperialist era was a time when monuments and memorials were erected in abundance, when jubilee celebrations and exhibitions were held for the same reason. The thousand-year commemoration of St Cyril and St Methodius, the 'apostles to the Slavs', for example, was the occasion for huge pan-Slav demonstrations and 'pilgrimages' of politicians and agitators from the Slav 'brother nations' to St Petersburg and Moscow. Hardly anyone was more assiduous and devoted than Lord Curzon in keeping the memory of British colonial achievement alive. National traditions of an imperialist stamp were particularly plentiful in Britain. In the tradition of the Holy Roman Empire, Germany possessed a starting-point for imperialist thinking. Italian imperialism was charged with the greatness of ancient Rome, but Britain too was inspired by the example of the Roman Empire and the Venetian state at the height of its power. The Musée de la France d'Outre Mer began its collection and exhibitions with the Crusades, which were interpreted also on other occasions in a French national and imperialist sense. Imperialist slogans like Pax Britannica, Pax

100 Monument to St Cyril and St Methodius in Novgorod called '1000 years in Russia'

Muscovita or the designation of 'proconsul' for the great custodians of British interests overseas all come from the arsenal of ancient history. The cult of the heroic, which was an integral part of the imperialist view of history, sought models not only in the distant past, but also in contemporary history.

It is contrary to the spirit of imperialism to cultivate history for its own sake and consciously to lose oneself in it. A movement filled with the present and directed towards the future uses the past only to arouse enthusiasm, to discover encouraging or admonitory examples to confirm itself. In this connection the title of Cramb's book, *The Origin and Destiny of Imperial Britain*, seems symptomatic. It was the 'law which brought us forth' that was sought in history, in order to fulfil it all the better in the future. Thus Seeley's historical lectures, as well as the imperialist visions of the future in Dilke's *Greater Britain*, the concluding passages of Prévost-Paradol's *La Nouvelle France*, the outlook in Danilevsky's *Russia and Europe* or Ukhtomsky's *Russo-Asiatic Musings*, must be seen in relation to these concepts of the time.

The physiognomy of the age of imperialism had, in general, optimistic features, yet there was no lack of cares and anxieties, and these had perhaps a greater influence on politics and the general mode of behaviour than at first appears. An English political writer, O. B. Bland, described this on the eve of the First World War: 'It is one of the penalties of the struggling materialism of the Western World, where nations of shop-keepers under armed guards worship the golden calves, that such ease and comfort as we enjoy, must ever be marred by apprehensions of impending danger.'

Those inclined towards biological or economic determinism found sufficient evidence of threatening developments. In the sense of a 'prophetic Malthusianism' there were widespread fears of the impending over-population of the world. Political anxieties about population were accompanied by a lively discussion on the alleged exhaustion of minerals and other supplies of raw materials in the not too distant future. The circulation of biological and eugenic racial theories, and some-times of hygienic improvements in the spirit of a so-called 'reform of life', cannot be separated from simultaneous fears of a general racial deterioration. The rise of a number of catch-words concerning 'danger' illuminates the spiritual condition of the epoch. A German writer, A. Wirth, remarked on this mentality among his countrymen:

> Formerly it was the French who made our blood boil; in recent times it is now the Americans, now the Red International, now the 'Gold International' that makes us tremble; now the Russian bear that tries to eat us up, now the English boa-constrictor that means to strangle us. The 'black' or 'brown' danger has been in fashion since the Herero War. . . . At present the huge 'Yellow Dragon' is worked up and threatens to darken our skies like a powerful comet. But even that is not the end.

101 Poster of 1894, showing French nostalgia for glories of the past ▶

NOUV^{es} AFFICHES ARTISTIQUES — G. DE MALHERBE & H A CELLOT RUE N-D DES CHAMPS 54

In his pamphlet, *The German Panic*, J. A. Hobson criticized the British for their susceptibility to similar slogans: France, Russia and Germany had been successively represented as England's 'natural enemies'. It was by no means only the imperialists, but also their opponents, who fell victim to one or the other of these fears; but there are good grounds for identifying the existence and political effectiveness of the above-mentioned misgivings as typical characteristics of the age of imperialism. Possibly incited by widely-read books such as *Le Péril National* (1888) or *Le Péril Financier* (1888), there was talk at least from the 1880s in France and Central Europe of an 'American peril', by which was meant the danger of the United States' outstripping Europe in economic competition. Then Vicomte de Vogüe, the French author, believed that he had discovered the 'America of the East' during a trip to Russia in 1884. He expressed this with a critical undertone: 'In our country we hear of nothing but the American danger.' But

102 French cartoon (1904) of 'the white peril' as seen in Asia: the German, the Russian, the Briton and the Frenchman

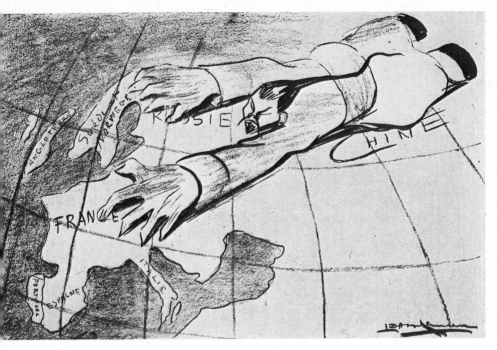

103 French cartoon (1904) of 'the yellow peril' as seen in Europe

Russia should likewise be considered. 'We shall not escape this Cossack invasion, the phantom of our fathers; only it will emerge in a modern form as agricultural and industrial oppression.'

The best known of all these catchphrases is 'the yellow peril' (probably fathered by the saying 'American peril'), which expressed a whole sheaf of threats at once. The workers in the 'white' countries feared the competition of coolies and being undercut by cheap labour with a minimum standard of living. The European and North American economies were concerned about the successes of Japanese production. Finally a picture was projected of the complete political emancipation of the large 'yellow' nations, who, armed with modern weapons and because of numerical superiority, would be able to clear the 'white man' out of the Far East and become masters of the East, perhaps even of the world. Linked with this was the thought of infiltration of areas formerly ruled by whites, not only through yellow workers, but also yellow farmers and settlers.

There were a good many more 'danger' slogans. Thus 'Africa for the Africans' was answered by a 'black peril' slogan and, conversely, the Far East soon began to speak of a 'European' or 'white' or 'Western' peril. Finally, it was only at a time when great politics had taken on world dimensions and people began to be concerned on a world scale with enemies, conspiracies, the creation of blocs and fronts, that the idea of a Zionist conspiracy to dominate the world could emerge and find credence. (The 'Protocols of the Elders of Zion' were evidently forged by the Russians about 1900.)

The socialist movement, however, counted among the actual threats to the imperialist world as a bourgeois-capitalist and power-political order. We are not so much concerned here with whether imperialists conceived of the Red International as a kind of conspiracy in the way people formerly regarded the Freemasons and the Jesuits, or whether they recognized it more accurately as the outward manifestation of social development. What was decisive in this context was that people felt threatened and not only considered but employed repressive as well as positive measures. Imperialism was very conscious of 'the social question', and many of the imperially-minded made both theoretical and practical attempts to effect compromises or seek new solutions in this area.

Power rivalry among the leading nations was not the least of imperialism's worries. The fear of being overreached, surpassed, crushed or encircled in one way or another constituted a powerful factor in the imperialist's attitude towards life, particularly among statesmen and the military. This was true whether one regarded a diplomatic and military conflict of empires as ultimately avoidable, or saw it as an elemental, inevitable and ever-existing basic fact of human cohabitation – transposed, to be sure, through technology, the increase of population, and the sophistication of social and political organization, to horrifying proportions.

104 The fears and aggressions that permeated Europe in the years before the First World War are expressed in this 1896 painting by Arnold Böcklin ▶

In the imperialist world-picture it was not only economic competition that held a firm position, but also the power competition of states, nations and races, and the involvement of war. This did not mean that the imperialist *eo ipso* had to relish war and include it as an unavoidable factor in his calculations. Nor was it the case that imperialist policy was forced by the inherent faults of the capitalist system to resort to war again and again in order to find a supposed way out of threatening social and economic chaos. But one thing is certainly true: that the imperialist concept of war was different from and more positive than the utilitarian-pacifist *Weltanschauung*. Many imperialists looked on war not so much as a not yet conquered holdover from a barbaric stage in man's history, but rather as (in Moltke's words) a 'link in God's world-design', the powerful motor of history which, though admittedly evil in many respects, was nevertheless a destiny to be accepted and prepared for. We have already discussed the status of the military in imperialist society. In terms of *Weltanschauung* and attitudes to life, this corresponded with the affirmation of war and the emphasis of its positive aspects without necessarily overlooking its horrors. Military service and war were praised as the basic education for character and life; war was presented as a 'bath of steel' and the opportunity for comprehensive regeneration; training and perfection in armed service was plainly regarded as every healthy man's duty to his fatherland.

A variant of the military mentality is the joy of adventure which could be sought within and outside military life. The appeal to the love of adventure counted among the strongest enticements; it ranged from the crudest to the most sublime forms, from garish posters urging men to join the colonial troops to the hidden motives of the heroes of imperialism. In the philosophy of Vitalism as in the nihilism of the political right, combat could attain the role of an end in itself or the highest value, but in the imperialist *Weltanschauung* war remained, as a rule, a means to an end. We can gather from the works of Kingsley, who took such a passionate interest in the Crimean War and cultivated friendships among the officers at Sandhurst, from Tennyson's poems and from Kipling's ballads, what was expected in Great Britain at that time from war service and the way it was believed warlike achievements could be interpreted. In his *Memoir of Hubert Hervey, Student and Imperialist*, Grey raised a memorial to the bellicose idealist. Cramb's philosophical justification of war seems to us like a combination of Neo-idealism, *Lebensphilosophie* and imperialism:

> War, therefore, I would define as a phase in the life-effort of the State towards complete self-realisation, a phase of the eternal nisus, the perpetual omnipotent strife of all being towards self-fulfilment. Destruction is not its aim, but the intensification of the life, whether of the conquering or the conquered State. War is thus a manifestation of the world-spirit in the form of man.

Especially favourable premises for the high esteem of the military existed in Germany as a result of the unusually strong military orientation of the Prussian social disposition, which encroached on the whole Hohenzollern Empire after 1870. We have already pointed out, however, that a predominance of the military organization in state and society did not necessarily imply a permanent threat of war against neighbouring states nor the conduct of war with them. Ideological utterances of the old Prussian military spirit remained essentially simpler and more modest than those of Wilhelmine imperialism, in which we can recognize fear of world competition as the empirical motive and Social Darwinism and Vitalism as the philosophical basis. The stirring experiences of 1914 and the years that followed produced a 'war philosophy' in other German philosophical schools. But Germany's defeat in the First World War silenced *this* kind of philosophy.

For the multitude of imperialist-thinking circles, observation of the power and prestige, the global expansion and other political successes of their countries offered sufficient satisfaction. Some groups, however, wanted more. They were not content with a crude national egoism as justification for imperialist modes of behaviour; they could not have a good conscience until they felt it possible to combine their expansive activities with missionary ideas and world tasks. Such messianic conceptions could be quite general and not very precise in detail: the protection and spread of humanity, of freedom, of Western culture. As a rule, however, imperialist ideologies had national tints: the French and Italian ideal of Latin civilization as a world aim, 'Der deutsche Gedanke in der Welt' (Rohrbach), the victory of a Protestant, liberal Anglo-Saxon civilization throughout the world simply in the service of justice and mankind.

Slavophile and pan-Slav ideologists spoke of the healing powers for all mankind which were supposed to be inherent in Slavdom, and combined these thoughts with hopes of a renewal of Christianity. The day of Slavdom, which was to begin when the hour of the Romano-Catholic and Germano-Protestant peoples ran out, took on a messianic significance for the world when seen in this light. If Christian viewpoints still played a big part in Russian imperialist thought, the world programmes of the other European countries were likewise based on thought structures of religious origins, but these had, almost without exception, been secularized in the age of imperialism and must be approached as typical ideologies. The religious periphery had not, of course, entirely disappeared. In this context we are not examining the content of reality in these ideologies but stressing the fact that intellectual contemporaries felt the need to prepare for themselves and their countries world tasks, in the fulfilment of which they saw the purpose of existence. According to Dilke, the possession of India offered Great Britain 'that

element of vastness of dominion which, in this age, is needed to secure width of thought and nobility of purpose'; and Curzon closed his discourse on India's place in the British Empire with the words: 'Remember first and foremost that India remains the great test of British character and heroism; a high grade of courage and a plenitude of worthy self-confidence must carry us forward and sustain us to the end of the road.' Such statements and admonitions reveal the longing to break away from every-day routine and lead an elevated existence whose content should be formed by dedication to a great cause.

We do not doubt the seriousness nor the genuineness of this line of thought and are entirely of the opinion that it could thoroughly imbue talented and enthusiastic people – particularly young ones – and be transformed into political reality. Perhaps it is that percentage of noble outlook (always quantitatively so small) in all social movements that permeates them like a leaven and first lends them dignity and stature. In any case it is important not to take this nobler part for the whole but to accept the reality in all its overwhelming banality.

XIV THE END OF AN EPOCH
AND ITS SIGNIFICANCE

As the terminal phase of the age of 'classical' imperialism and the transition to a new epoch the First World War proves to be particularly illuminating for the *ultima ratio* of imperialism. The climax of European expansion across the earth that was reached by imperialism continually created new sources of conflict. However, the tensions and disputes which arose *outside* Europe could still be peacefully settled or bridged over, from the Berlin Congo Conference of 1884–85 up to 1914. But that was not the end of it. International politics was Janus-faced: there were efforts not only to reduce existing differences on the basis of agreements, but also to build up effective attack systems in the event that peaceful solutions seemed no longer attainable. Partly in the form of security pacts and alliances, partly through more or less binding agreements, the powers created European and world fronts, coalitions whose maintenance and strengthening became the supreme aim of their policies. It is obviously of considerable historical interest to ascertain what events and decisions in 1914 led to the outbreak of the First World War. With regard to the power structure of the epoch, however, it is no less important to recognize how much the existence of two large blocs determined the relations among the European states from the turn of the century. There were frequent attempts to loosen the rigid fronts. No one can say how things might have developed if, for example, Germany had been prepared to make generous concessions on the question of naval armament. On the contrary it can be said with certainty that the time was never ripe between 1894 and 1914 for a 'diplomatic revolution' or a 'renversement des alliances'. In a relatively short period, schools of diplomacy, foreign policy traditions and propaganda centres had been formed, all of which fitted into the bloc-building of the time. The alliance and *entente* systems could no longer be interchanged at the pleasure of cabinet policies in the pre-1914 era; they had become so firmly rooted in the public mind that it would have taken enormous efforts to become free of them. This general line of major policy must be seen in connection with the increasing social fermentation and the spiritual trends of the period (as we have tried to sketch them in their imperialist aspect), in order to recognize how dangerous the situation had become.

Once the war broke out, the violent and destructive aspects of imperialism began to dominate, whereas previously its progressive side had also been evident throughout. A wild, fanatic and senseless form of nationalism, which the imperialist movement had at times overshadowed but never eliminated, erupted everywhere. Yet again, and once more, war proved itself as a reality not yet to be dispensed with although many people were already maintaining its avoidability and regarding it as an obsolete method of settling international disputes. In association with the excesses of nationalism there were immediately paroxysms of militarism. In the war aims and post-war planning which soon set in, use was made of the traditional arsenal of power-politics concepts: the dissolution of existing empires; annexations; future long-term suppression of the enemy after victory; the creation of new zones of influence and the extension of existing ones; designs for hegemony.

On the other hand, it is impressive to see how much war, and particularly *this* war, stimulated the spirit of scientific discovery and technical invention. The adequate supply of arms and ammunition to the troops, food and other provisions for the army and the civilian population, mass transport of men and equipment, the overcoming of shortages, and financing the war – all these problems taxed the organizational powers of govern-ments and administrations as never before. As a rule one enters upon war with a store of experience from a previous war, but it soon becomes evident that the situation has changed; and he who makes the quickest adaptation has already gained a decisive lead. One of the war's contributions to the expansion of modernity (and in its questionable attributes at that) was the establishment of increasingly intensive political propaganda abroad and at home. No state can do without propaganda any longer; the situation in which this need became evident and its mastery indispensable was war – the life and death struggle. The war also caused conspicuous upheavals in the areas of social structure and internal politics. Efforts against the external enemy had to be effected through concessions at home which the ruling classes would have granted with infinitely more reluctance in peacetime. In Germany the Social Democrat opposition, under the stress of the outbreak of war, supported the government for the first time and, on the other hand, trade

105 French propaganda against the Central Powers at the beginning of the First World War

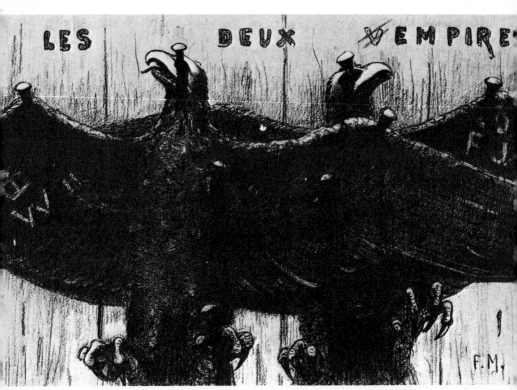

ANY MORE TO COME ?

GERMANY

AUSTRIA

106 British propaganda against Germany and Austria at the beginning of
the First World War

union representatives were officially drawn into cooperation in
organizational tasks. Conservative circles hoped, of course, that
military victory would preserve their political predominance;
but imminent defeat, the pressure exercised by President
Wilson, and a seething population rendered such hopes
illusory. At the eleventh hour the monarchical leopard tried to
change its spots: the Kaiser (in his capacity as King of Prussia)
and his government had no choice but to abandon the three-
class electoral system in Prussia, and in the last month of his
reign the Reich was given a parliamentary constitution.
Incomparably more significant in terms of world history was
the fact that the Russian Revolution and the eventual success
of its resulting political system had been made possible and
brought about by the war. The First World War, as the   185

"Lest we Forget"

Satan II.

High Priest of "Kultur."

Kaiser—"Woe and Death to all who oppose My Will."

Copyrighted and Pub'd by F. E. Lockwood, Argyle St., Derby.

quintessence of European great-power imperialist policy, was conducted in an orgy of nationalism and militarism, traditional power politics and concepts of rivalry; yet at the same time it contained much that pointed to the future rather than the past.

Movements as powerful and effective as imperialism do not disappear from the stage of history. Thus the First World War did not in any way signify the end of imperialism as a political mode of action or ideology. Influential circles in Great Britain perceived the result of the war as an incentive to continue and build up their imperial policies; in France the idea of 'l'Empire français' actually had its greatest boom between the wars, and on the Continent the Third Republic tried to strengthen its hegemony. Italian imperialism, which could boast of only minor successes before 1914, swelled to much more considerable proportions under Mussolini's leadership. Fascist Italy's aim of becoming the first power in the Mediterranean,

107, 108 Postcards in the service of war-time propaganda. Left, a British view of the Kaiser as Satan II. Right, 'May God punish England'; notice the change of the English to the German Channel

187

by means of a colonial empire in North and East Africa, was to a great extent realized. The strength acquired by Mussolini's policy up to 1941 (which astonishes us today) should be attributed more to the dictator's initiative and his tactical and propaganda dexterity than to the actual power of his country. But what is interesting in our context is that Italy attained the peak of its imperialist phase only after the First World War. Hitler's Reich succeeded for a few years in expanding into an all-Europe *imperium*: its excessive and self-destructive imperialism forced a number of European countries into a kind of colonial status. And just as 'dollar imperialism' did not die out with the First World War, so there were good reasons for coining the concept of 'Soviet imperialism'. Under Stalin, Russia was in a position to pursue imperialistic policies which went much farther than anything the Tsarist Empire had ever managed to achieve.

Non-Marxist historians do not usually characterize the epoch following the First World War as imperialistic although there is no doubt that all the great powers continued their imperialist policies after 1918. There are a number of arguments to justify this. In the first years after the end of the war, Russia was exhausted by revolution and civil war; true enough, it developed a world-revolution initiative, but not at first an imperialist one in the world-political sense. The United States, having repudiated President Wilson, tried to withdraw into political isolationism, even though this did not succeed. If foreign policy was to be determined by public interest and the most pregnant events, then the world was again faced with a Eurocentric situation. The tendency to divide up the colonial world had reached its zenith, after the partition of the Ottoman Empire and the German colonies had reinforced the influence of Great Britain and France overseas. Even if the imperialist states continued their economic expansion, territorial aggrandizement had come to a halt, until the ambitions of Japan, and later Italy and Germany, led again to a more turbulent era. The successful self-assertion of Turkey, Spain's defeat at Anual, the long resistance of Abd el-Krim, the persistent unrest in India, and the admission of Asiatic and African states into the League of Nations heralded the emancipation of the Afro-Asian world and introduced movements contrary to imperialism. The conversion of the British Empire into a Commonwealth and the granting of independence to members of the British 'family of nations' made steady progress.

At the beginning of this book we spoke of the conceptual determination of imperialism and of the motives which may have led to its rise. Now, at the end, it remains to make the reader acquainted with those interpretations which are supposed to explain the significance of imperialism in the context of world history. The conceptions of contemporary imperialists in their own time, and the nature of their hopes for the future and their programmes, have already been discussed. Nor will we consider here the findings of the lively British study of imperialism since the 1950s (Robinson, Gallagher, Stokes, Fieldhouse, MacDonagh, Semmel, Thornton) or of Galbraith in the United States. These scholars, claiming the general validity of the classical British model, have studied Formal and Informal Empire, Imperialism and Anti-imperialism of Free Trade, Forward School and Consolidationist School of Imperialism, and they have achieved extremely illuminating results.

John A. Hobson stands out as representative of an important group of interpreters and critics of imperialism as an international phenomenon, and his book *Imperialism* ranks with the world literature of politics. He considers the nation a healthy basis for political existence. Like all Liberals of his time he holds the national idea in high esteem, but it is not a supreme value in his thinking, rather a transitional stage or, more correctly, an element in the ordering of world peace and for a future League of Nations. Hobson's actual point of departure, however, is neither nation nor state but economic life, and he had very decided views on the only correct way to organize it. Hobson

189

was a convinced Free Trader, but broadened the Free Trade programme, on the grounds of social-liberal, semi-socialist demands, to state control of the economy and a more just distribution of the national income: a 'social reform' whose primary purpose was 'to raise the wholesome standard of private and public consumption for a nation'. Domestic markets, he maintained, were capable of unlimited expansion. In contrast, he reduced imperialism to the common denominator of the search for markets for overproduction caused by the lack of sufficient home consumption, and the necessity to invest surplus capital. Since it seemed to Hobson that general concepts of political economy and official policy had already been more 'advanced' in the past than when he put pen to paper, he was able to characterize imperialist policy as plainly retrogressive; even more, the epoch appeared to him to contain the danger of degeneration, a relapse into barbarism. He admitted freely that certain vested interests got full value out of an imperialist system: particular export industries, the armaments industry, shipbuilding and shipping, railroad construction, canal construction, military men and diplomats to whom imperialism offered increased opportunities of advancement, and above all, investment capital. In this context, he follows with fierce attacks against international finance capital. His conclusion: imperialism devours immense sums for unproductive purposes, particularly armaments, and imperialist policy continually increases the risk of war. A safety-valve for over-population was not necessary. Great Britain was not over-populated and the population would reach a stationary level about the middle of the century. The claim that Britain brought freedom to the underdeveloped peoples was untrue; rather, the British character and methods of government overseas assumed an unfavourable autocratic trait, and it was to be feared that this despotic strain would have repercussions on the internal politics of Britain itself. The gravest danger lay in the fact that the nation might, through imperialism, reach a frame of mind which made it incapable of self-criticism.

Thus Hobson wants to demonstrate that imperialism, seen as a whole, represents the penetration of modern economic society by an anti-economic, parasitic principle. An age which subscribes to imperialism must show reactionary and anachronistic features. Political ambition, lust for adventure and chauvinism in the imperialist system appeared to him to disturb and endanger a rational economic development. Hobson subtitled his book 'A Study of Social Pathology' in later editions.

Virtually all the leading Marxist intellectuals have also concerned themselves intensively with the phenomenon of imperialism. They too begin from the social-economic situation and readily adopt a large part of the research of their liberal forerunners, as, for example, Lenin did in his *Imperialism, the Highest Stage of Capitalism*. Their conclusions, however, are characteristically turned about. What Hobson sees as an aberration, an anachronism, an incursion of viewpoints alien to economics, Lenin perceives as the logical, necessary consequence of social and economic processes as expounded in Marxist theory. Within a capitalist economy, banking capital changes from a relatively servile power to dominating finance capital. The rule of monopolies and the international financial oligarchy has begun. As a consequence of this, imperialism marks the catastrophic final phase of bourgeois society. Capitalism as a social system of individual countries has after all already broken down. But in order to postpone the end, capitalism turns aggressively abroad and hopes, through the conquest of foreign markets and the exploitation of foreign peoples, to prolong its life. The competitive struggle over the allotment of the part of the world that has not yet been securely seized – the 'non-capitalist world-milieu', as Rosa Luxemburg called it – the war of the imperialists against one another for world hegemony has begun and will pass over into the proletarian world-revolution.

Within the obligatory limits of the Marxist general line, the interpretations of socialist and communist writers differ considerably in detail. The opinions expressed on imperialism during the First World War by the orthodox Marxist Karl Kautsky seem to be of special interest. He feared that the capitalists might realize that the war must destroy capitalism, and that they might therefore decide on a peaceful exploitation of the world and unite. Kautsky coined the term 'ultra-imperialism' to describe this capitalist world plan, conducted and directed by finance capital with its international links. Kautsky was convinced that if a concept of this magnitude came about, the collapse of capitalism would be further postponed.

Soon after the victory of Bolshevism in Russia, attacks from the standpoint of economic liberalism were launched against the Marxist interpretation of imperialism. The name of the sociologist and economic historian, Joseph A. Schumpeter, a noteworthy critic of Marxism, may stand here as representative of many other scholars. Above all, Schumpeter sought to refute Lenin's thesis that imperialism was the inevitable consequence of capitalism. For this purpose he undertook a comprehensive *tour d'horizon* of universal history, in which, to be sure, the professional historian cannot always follow him. His conclusion is that there is indeed an economic root to imperialism, the formation of tariff-based trusts and cartels which lead to monopoly capitalism with monopolistic price-policies, to dumping and capital exports, and finally to aggressive economic policies and imperialist policies of expansion and conquest. *But* – protective tariffs, trusts and cartels do not spring from the automatism of competitive economy; rather they are the expression of political action with its roots in the pre-capitalist mercantile principalities. Thus imperialism is neither a necessary phase nor a development out of capitalism. Capitalism is anti-imperialist by its nature. Schumpeter defined it as 'the objectless inclination of a state towards forcible expansion without defined limits'.

The starting-point of Hannah Arendt's concern with imperialism is quite different from those of Hobson, Lenin and Schumpeter. Out of the painful experience of totalitarianism she seeks its origins and comes up against imperialism along the way. In order to explain it, she proves to be dependent on the economic-Marxist interpretation: for her the origin of imperialism is 'The existence of a small capitalist class whose fortunes exploded the social fabric of their countries and whose production capacity burst open the economic systems of their peoples, and who therefore scoured the world with greedy eyes to find profitable investments for their surplus capital.' In contrast to Schumpeter, who sees in imperialism a general historical phenomenon recurring from the earliest times right up to the present, though now increasingly anachronistic, Hannah Arendt considers it something new. A banal and shabby novelty, to be sure: 'a curious amalgam of capitalist export, racial madness and the grinding machinery of red tape', something without genuine imperial grandeur and worlds away from the greatness of the classical *imperia*. Despite all her borrowings of economic interpretation, Hannah Arendt is concerned first and last with totalitarianism. And this is primarily a social-political phenomenon that can by no means be explained exclusively through economics. Hannah Arendt's exposition of the dialectic between nationalism and imperialism is of considerable importance. The people and the statesmen of the time knew that class war had rent the very body of the nation, thus bringing the whole political and social framework into extreme danger. Expansion seemed to provide a common aim which would restore the country's unity. The imperialists became such dangerous domestic enemies simply because, as Hobson said, 'they were patriotic parasites' nourishing themselves on the genuine concern for the nation's continued existence felt by all true patriots. The imperialists held up to the people's eyes what seemed to be common and unalterable aims for their existence and welfare and 'this was the reason why European nationalists fell such extraordinarily easy victims to the imperialist infection whose cardinal principles were so resolutely opposed to their own'.

There can be no doubt that economic expansion constituted a considerable part of the whole imperialist phenomenon. All

193

the same it does not appear correct to interpret the epoch primarily from the economic angle. We proceed rather from the general change of consciousness within society and its influence on the interdependence of power politics, economics, and ideology. Of similar significance for the development of imperialism, however, seems to be the concept of the European nation-states as competitive and rival political factors. At the beginning of this book we attempted to define imperialism and, before describing the age of imperialism itself, to ascertain the causes of the international imperialist movement which emerged in the 1880s. We believed the answer to lie in the culmination of nationalism, the building of European national states and the sharpening of global competition between the great powers. The interpretation of the universal-historical function of the imperialist age must also move in this direction: such interpretations are, of course, the furthest a historian working empirically dares to go beyond the limits of his descriptive, critical and analytical tasks.

On the one hand we can perceive in imperialism, as a consequence of the increased participation of the people and the growing influence of public opinion, a further important contribution to the continuing democratization of national politics. On the other hand imperialism presents itself as a coalescence of state and economy, as an alliance of power politics with the industrial revolution and the technical boom of the nineteenth and twentieth centuries. Imperialism also signifies the establishment of an age of world politics. Of course the methods and means by which world politics were conducted at that time (dividing up the world into possessions and spheres of interest of the consolidated national states, the translation of national-state into world-political rivalries) are no longer acceptable today. The great problems of our own times have become even more a matter of universal mankind than in the epoch discussed here, and the methods of imperialism have proved inadequate to solve them. We must not, however, overlook the fact that the policy of national egoism was already superseded in many respects by the imperialist foundation of empires and commonwealths. Finally we cannot deny the tremendous achievement of opening up the world, which was bound up with imperialist expansion and which contributed to the birth of Afro-Asian emancipation. Imperialism is certainly not identical with colonialism, but what H. Lüthy said in *Colonization and the Making of Mankind* applies to the imperialist phenomenon as a whole:

> The content of the history of colonization is not the rise and fall of colonial empires, the political domination of foreign countries; these have always been transitory. It is, and has been from the beginning of history, the tremendous process by which the world was discovered, opened to man, and settled; the process by which roads, coasts and oceans were made accessible and safe, by which closed continents, forbidden kingdoms and isolated societies were forced open or broken up by new expanding forces, new techniques, new customs, new knowledge, and new forms of social organization. It might be said that the history of colonization is the history of humanity itself.

Despite its considerable reactionary tendencies and impulses we regard the age of imperialism as a whole neither as a relapse nor an anachronism, but rather as an epoch of positive significance for the attainment and the future of 'One World'.

SELECT BIBLIOGRAPHY

GENERAL HISTORY 1880–1914

Barraclough, G.   *An Introduction to Contemporary History*, London 1964.

Dhombres, P.   *Les relations internationales de 1870 à nos jours*, v. I: 1870–1914. Paris 1946.

Hayes, C.J.H.   *Contemporary Europe since 1870*. New York 1964 (4th edn.).

Histoire générale des civilisations, v. VI: *Le XIXe siècle, L'apogée de l'expansion européenne, 1815–1914*. Paris 1955.

Historia Mundi, v. X: *Das 19. und 20. Jahrhundert*. Bern/Munich 1961

Lüthy, H.   'Colonization and the Making of Mankind' in *Journal of Economic History*, XXI, pp. 483–95.

Mansergh, N.   *The Coming of the First World War, A Study in the European Balance, 1878–1914*. London 1949.

The New Cambridge Modern History, v. XI: *Material Problems and World-Wide Problems*. Cambridge 1962; v. XII: *The Era of Violence*. Cambridge 1960.

Propyläen Weltgeschichte, v. VIII: *Das neunzehnte Jahrhundert*. Berlin 1960; v. IX: *Das zwanzigste Jahrhundert*. Berlin 1960.

Renouvin, P.   *La Crise européenne et la première guerre mondiale, 1904–1918*. Paris 1962 (4th edn.).

Seton-Watson, R.W.   *Britain in Europe, 1789–1914, A survey of foreign policy*. Cambridge 1937.

Schieder, T. (ed.)   *Handbuch der europäischen Geschichte*, v.

VI: *Europa im Zeitalter der National-staaten und europäischen Weltpolitik bis zum Ersten Weltkrieg.* Stuttgart 1968.

THE HISTORY OF IMPERIALISM

Barraclough, G.	'Das europäische Gleichgewicht und der neue Imperialismus' in *Propyläen Weltgeschichte*, v. VIII, pp. 703–39.
Bourgin, G.	*Les politiques de l'expansion impérialiste.* Paris 1949.
Brown, M. B.	*After Imperialism.* London 1963.
Friedjung, H.	*Das Zeitalter des Imperialismus, 1884–1914*, 3 vols. Berlin 1919–22.
Gollwitzer, H.	*Die Gelbe Gefahr, Geschichte eines Schlagworts.* Studien zum imperialistischen Denken, Göttingen 1962.
Hallgarten, G. W. F.	*Imperialismus vor 1914, Die soziologischen Grundlagen der Aussenpolitik europäischer Grossmächte bis 1914*, 2 vols. Munich 1963 (2nd edn.).
Koebner, R. and Schmidt, H. Dan.	*Imperialism, The Story and Significance of a Political Word, 1840–1960.* Cambridge 1964.
Langer, W. L.	*The Diplomacy of Imperialism, 1890–1902.* Cambridge, Mass. 1960 (2nd edn.).
Meyer, E. *et al.*	*Europa und der Kolonialismus.* Zürich/Stuttgart 1962.
Rein, G. A.	*Die europäische Ausdehnung über die Erde.* Berlin 1931.
Schüssler, W. (ed.)	*Weltmachtstreben und Flottenbau.* Witten (Ruhr) 1956.
Snyder, L. L. (ed.)	*The Imperialism Reader, Documents and*

	readings in modern expansionism. Princeton 1962.
Sternberg, F.	*Der Imperialismus.* Berlin 1926.
Strachey, J.	*The End of Empire.* London 1959.
Taylor, A.J.P.	*The Struggle for Mastery in Europe, 1848–1918.* Oxford 1954.
Thornton, A.P.	*The Imperial Idea and Its Enemies.* London 1959.

POPULATION

Kuczynski, R.R.	*Population Movements.* Oxford 1936.
MacKenroth, G.	*Bevölkerungslehre.* Berlin/Göttingen/ Heidelberg 1952.
Myrdal, G.	*Population, A Problem for Democracy.* Oxford 1940.
Reinhard, M.R. and Armengaud, A.	*Histoire générale de la population mondiale* Paris 1961.

IMPERIALISM AND NATIONALISM

d'Assac, J.P.	*Doctrines du nationalisme.* La librairie française, Paris 1958.
Chadwick, H.M.	*The Nationalities of Europe and the Growth of National Ideologies.* Cambridge 1966 (2nd edn.).
Dockhorn, K.	*Die Staatsphilosophie des englischen Idealismus, Ihre Lehre und Wirkung.* Bochum 1937.
Fischel, A.	*Der Panslavismus bis zum Weltkreig.* Stuttgart/Berlin 1919.
Hertz, F.O.	*Nationality in History and Politics, A study of the psychology and sociology of*

	national sentiment and character. London 1944.
Kohn, H.	*The Age of Nationalism, The First Era of Global History.* New York 1962. *Panslavism, Its history and ideology.* Notre Dame, Indiana 1953.
Lemberg, E.	*Geschichte des Nationalismus in Europa.* Stuttgart 1950.
Playne, C. E.	*The Pre-War Mind in Britain.* London 1928.
Snyder, L. L.	*The Dynamics of Nationalism, Readings in its meaning and development.* Princeton 1964.
Sulzbach, W.	*Imperialismus und Nationalbewusstsein.* Frankfurt 1959.

SOCIAL IMPERIALISM

Cole, M.	*The Story of Fabian Socialism.* London 1961.
Grabowsky, A.	*Der Sozialimperialismus als letzte Etappe des Imperialismus.* Forschungen sur Weltpolitik und Weltwirtschaft, v. I. Basel 1939.
MacDonald, R.	*Labour and the Empire.* London 1907.
Naumann, F.	*Werke,* 5 vols. Cologne/Opladen 1964–7.
Semmel, B.	*Imperialism and Social Reform, English social-imperial thought, 1895–1914.* London 1960.
Weber, M.	*Gesammelte Aufsätze sur Soziologie und Sozialpolitik.* Tübingen 1924.

ENGLAND

Bodelsen, C. A.	*Studies in Mid-Victorian Imperialism.* London 1960.

The Cambridge History of the British Empire, v. III. Cambridge 1959.

Hutchins, F. G.	*The Illusion of Permanence, British Imperialism in India.* Princeton 1967.
Marder, A. J.	*The Anatomy of British Sea Power, 1880–1905.* London 1964 (2nd edn.).
Mommsen, W. J.	'Nationale und ökonomische Faktoren im britischen Imperialismus vor 1914' in *Historische Zeitschrift*, Band 206 (1968), pp. 618–64.
Pribram, A. F.	*England and the International Policy of the European Great Powers, 1871–1914.* Oxford 1931.
Robinson, R., Gallagher, J. and Denny, A.	*Africa and the Victorians, The official mind of imperialism.* London 1961.
Seton-Watson, R. W.	*Disraeli, Gladstone and the Eastern Question.* London 1935.
Tyler, J. E.	*The Struggle for Imperial Unity, 1868–1895.* London 1938.

FRANCE

Brunschwig, H.	*Myths and Realities of French Colonialism, 1871–1914.* London 1966.
Deschamps, H.	*Les Méthodes et les doctrines coloniales de la France du XVIe siècle a nos jours.* Paris 1953.
Julien, C. A.	'Jules Ferry' in *Les politiques d'expansion impérialiste*, pp. 11–72. Paris 1949.

201

Power, T. F.   *Jules Ferry and the Renaissance of French Imperialism.* New York 1944.

Roberts, S. H.   *History of French Colonial Policy, 1870–1925,* 2 vols. London 1929.

Sieberg, H.   *Eugène Etienne und die französische Kolonialpolitik, 1887–1904.* Cologne/Opladen 1968.

GERMANY

Dawson, W. H.   *The German Empire, 1867–1914, and the Unity Movement.* Oxford 1966 (2nd edn.).

Jerussalimski, A. S.   *Der deutsche Imperialismus.* Berlin 1968.

Ritter, G.   'Die Hauptmächte Europas und das Wilhelminische Reich, 1896–1914' in *Staatskunst und Kriegshandwerk,* v. II. Munich 1960.

Townsend, M. E.   *The Rise and Fall of Germany's Colonial Empire, 1884–1918.* New York 1930.

RUSSIA

Hoetzsch, O. (ed.)   *Die internationalen Beziehungen im Zeitalter des Imperialismus, Dokumente aus den Archiven der zaristischen und provisorischen Regierung, 1878–1917.* Berlin 1931.

Hoetzsch, O.   *Russland in Asien, Geschichte einer Expansion.* Stuttgart 1966.

Seton-Watson, H.   *Decline of Imperial Russia, 1855–1914.* London 1952.

Sumner, B. H.   *Tsardom and Imperialism in the Far East and Middle East, 1880–1914.* London 1942.

Adler, M. and
Hilferding, R.

Das Finanzkapital, Eine Studie über die jüngste Entwicklung des Kapitalismus (1910). Marx-Studien, v. III. Vienna 1923.

Arendt, H.

The Origins of Totalitarianism. New York 1951, London 1958.

Barnes, H. E.

World Politics in Modern Civilization, The contributions of nationalism, imperialism and militarism to human culture and international anarchy. New York 1930.

Brailsford, O. H. N.

The War of Steel and Gold. London 1914.

Bukharin, N. I.

Der Imperialismus und die Akkumulation des Kapitals. Vienna/Berlin 1926.

Fieldhouse, D. K.

The Theory of capitalist imperialism. London 1967.

Hobhouse, L. T.

Democracy and Reaction. London 1904.

Hobson, J. A.

Imperialism, A Study (1902). London 1961 (6th edn.).

Kautsky, K.

'Der Imperialismus' in *Die Neue Zeit* XXXII (1914), pp. 908–22.
Nationalstaat, imperialisticher Staat und Staatenbund. Nuremberg 1915.

Kemp, T.

Theories of Imperialism. London 1968.

Lenin, V. I.

Imperialism, the Highest Stage of Capitalism. Moscow 1947.

Lukács, G.

Die Zerstörung der Vernunft, Der Weg des Irrationalismus von Schelling zu Hitler. Berlin 1955.

Luxemburg, R.

The Accumulation of Capital. London 1963.

Nemmers, E. E.

Hobson and Underconsumption. Amsterdam 1956.

Schumpeter, J. A.	*Capitalism, Socialism and Democracy.* New York 1942, London 1950 (3rd edn.).
Seillière, E. A. A. L.	*La philosophie de l'impérialisme*, 4 vols. Paris 1903–8.
Varga, E. and Mendelsohn, L.	*New Data for V.I. Lenin's 'Imperialism, the Highest Stage of Capitalism'.* London 1939, New York 1940.
Winslow, E. M.	'Marxian, Liberal, and Sociological Theories of Imperialism' in *The Journal of Political Economy* 39 (1931). *The Pattern of Imperialism, A Study in the Theories of Power.* New York 1948.

IMPERIALIST IDEOLOGY

Chamberlain, H. St.	*Die Grundlagen des 19. Jahrhunderts.* Munich 1899.
Cramb, J. A.	*The Origins and Destiny of Imperial Britain* (1900). London 1915.
Danilevski, N. Y.	*Rossiya i Evropa.* St Petersburg 1871. (German translation: *Russland und Europa.* Stuttgart/Berlin 1920.)
Delbruck, H.	*Vor und nach dem Kriege, Politische und historische Aufsätze, 1902–1925.* Berlin 1926.
Dilke, C.	*Problems of Greater Britain*, 2 vols. London/New York 1890.
Fadeyev, R. A.	*Opinion on the Eastern Question* (1871). London 1876 (2nd edn.).
Gobineau, A.	*Essai sur l'inégalité des races humaines*, 4 vols. Paris 1853–5. (English translation: *The Inequality of Human Races.* London 1915.)

Gumplowicz, L.   *Der Rassenkampf, Soziologische Unter-*
                    suchungen. Innsbruck 1883.

Hanotaux, G. A. A. *Histoire de la France contemporaine, 1871–*
                    1900, 4 vols. Paris 1903–8.

Haushofer, K. *et al.* *Bausteine zur Geopolitik.* Berlin 1928.

Kjellén, R.   *Die Grossmächte der Gegenwart.* Leipzig/
                    Berlin 1914.

MacKinder, H. J.   *Britain and the British Seas* (1902). Oxford
                    1930 (2nd revised edn.).
                    The Scope and Methods of Geography and
                    the Geographical Pivot of History (1904).
                    London 1951.

Marcks, E.   *Die imperialistische Idee in der Gegenwart.*
                    Dresden 1903.

Peters, C.   *Gesammelte Schriften* (ed. W. Frank),
                    4 vols. Berlin 1943–4.

Ratzel, F.   *Politische Geographie* (1897). Munich/
                    Berlin 1903.

Ratzenhofer, G.   *Wesen und Zweck der Politik, als Theil*
                    der Sociologie und Grundlage der Staats-
                    wissenschaften, 3 vols. Leipzig 1893.

Rohrbach, P.   *Der deutsche Gedanke in der Welt.* Düssel-
                    dorf/Leipzig 1912.

Seeley, J. R.   *The Expansion of England.* Cambridge
                    1883.

Spengler, O.   *The Decline of the West.* New York/
                    London 1934.

Wilkinson, S.   *The Nation's Awakening.* London 1896.

ECONOMIC CONDITIONS OF IMPERIALISM

Baumont, M.   *L'Essor industriel et l'impérialisme colonial,*
                    1878–1904. Paris 1965 (3rd edn.).

Bickel, W.   'Wirtschaftliche Aspekte des Kolonialismus im Zeitalter des Imperialismus und in der Gegenwart' in *Europa und der Kolonialismus*. Zürich/Stuttgart 1962.

Clark, G.   *The Balance Sheets of Imperialism*. New York 1967 (2nd edn.).

Dobb, M. H.   *Studies in the Development of Capitalism*. London 1946.

Edwards, G. W.   *The Evolution of Finance Capitalism*. New York/London 1938.

Feis, H.   *Europe, the World's Banker, 1870–1914*. New Haven 1930.

Gallagher, J. and Robinson, R.   'The Imperialism of Free Trade' in *The Economic History Review*, Second Series, v. VI (1953), pp. 1–15.

Halévy, E.   *Imperialism and the Rise of Labour*. New York 1961.

Hancock, W. K.   *The Wealth of Colonies*, Cambridge 1950.

Hoffman, R. J. S.   *Great Britain and the German Trade Rivalry, 1875–1914*. Philadelphia/Oxford 1933.

Imlah, A.   *Economic Elements in the Pax Britannica*. Cambridge, Mass. 1958.

Macdonagh, O.   'The Anti-Imperialism of Free Trade' in *The Economic History Review*, Second Series, v. XIV (1962), pp. 489–501.

Miller, M. S.   *Economic Development of Russia, 1905–1914*. London 1926.

Robbins, L.   *The Theory of Economic Policy in English Classical Political Economy*. London 1952.

Rostow, W. W.   *The Process of Economic Growth*. Oxford 1960.

	Stages of Economic Growth, A Non-Communist Manifesto. Cambridge 1960.
Staley, E.	*War and the Private Investor.* New York 1935.
Sweezy, P.M.	*The Theory of Capitalist Development, Principles of Marxian Political Economy.* London 1946.
Winch, D.	*Classical Political Economy and Colonies.* London 1965.

SOCIAL AND CULTURAL ASPECTS OF IMPERIALISM

Carroll, E.M.	*French Public Opinion and Foreign Affairs, 1870–1914.* New York 1931. *Germany and the Great Powers, 1866–1914, A Study of Public Opinion and Foreign Policy.* New York 1938.
Hale, O.J.	*Publicity and Diplomacy, with special reference to England and Germany, 1890–1914.* New York 1940.
Hitchcock, H.R.	*Architecture: Nineteenth and Twentieth Centuries.* Harmondsworth 1958.
Kehr, E.	*Schlachtflottenbau und Parteipolitik, 1894–1901.* Berlin 1930.
Masur, G.	*Prophets of Yesterday, Studies in European Culture, 1890–1914.* London 1963.
Schieder, T.	'Political and Social Developments in Europe' in *The New Cambridge Modern History*, v. XI, pp. 243–73.
Schumpeter, J.A.	*Imperialism and Social Classes* (1919). Oxford 1951.
Vagts, A.	*A History of Militarism.* New York 1938.

LIST OF ILLUSTRATIONS

1 Design for an imperial palace for the sovereigns of the British Empire, J.M. Gandy, 1834. Royal Academy of Arts, London

2 Design for new Houses of Parliament, J.M. Gandy, 1836. Royal Academy of Arts, London

3 Binding of *Travels in the East of Nicholas II*, by E. Ukhtomsky, Russian edition, 1895–96. British Museum. Photo: Freeman

4 Russia and Britain in Asia; cartoon from *Figaro*, Vienna 1894. Photo: Freeman

5 *The Oath at Versailles*, painting by Anton von Werner, 1871. British Museum. Photo: Freeman

6 The Royal Exchange, London, *c.* 1896. Photo: Radio Times Hulton Picture Library

7 Friedrichstrasse Railway Station, Berlin, *c.* 1905. Photo: Ullstein Bilderdienst, Berlin

8 The Triumph of Steam and Electricity; from the *Illustrated London News*, 1897. Photo: Freeman

9 Advances in transport: the bicycle. French poster, 1894. Musée des Arts Décoratifs, Paris

10 Advances in transport: the automobile. French poster, 1902. Musée des Arts Décoratifs, Paris

11 Advances in transport: the air traffic of the future. Caricature from *L'Assiette au Beurre*, Paris, 1901. Photo: Freeman

12 Cartoon on Bismarck from *Kladderadatsch*, Berlin, 1875. Photo: Freeman

13 The Triple Alliance; cartoon from *Kladderadatsch*, Berlin, 1883. Photo: Freeman

14 British troops at the Pyramids, 1882. Photo: Radio Times Hulton Picture Library

15 *The Sword of Damocles* (Russo-Japanese relations); cartoon from *L'Assiette au Beurre*, Paris, 1903. Photo: Freeman

16 British and American attitude to the Russo-Japanese conflict; Russian postcard, *c.* 1902. British Museum. Photo: Freeman

17 The Franco-Russian military alliance: French caricature, 1894. British Museum. Photo: Freeman

18 The Moroccan dispute; cartoon from *L'Assiette au Beurre*, 1903. Photo: Freeman

19 Illustration from *Pictures for Little Englanders* by R. A. Foster, 1876. British Museum. Photo: Freeman

20 Vignette from *Slavische Blätter*, Vienna, 1865. British Museum. Photo: Freeman

21 The Pan-Slav Congress in Moscow; cartoon from *Figaro*, Vienna, 1867. British Museum. Photo: Freeman

22 Title-page of Danilevsky's *Russia and Europe*, 1888. Photo: Freeman

23 The Tsarevich at the Pyramids; photograph from Ukhtomsky's *Travels in the East of Nicholas II*, 1895–96 ed. Photo: Freeman

24 The harbour of Vladivostok. Photo: Radio Times Hulton Picture Library

25 Charles Dilke, pen and ink drawing by H. Furness. National Portrait Gallery

26 James Froude, by J. Goodall. National Portrait Gallery

27 Napoleon III, detail of painting by Flandrin, Château du Versailles. Photo: Giraudon, Paris

28 Algiers, *c.* 1905. Photo: H. Roger Viollet, Paris

29 Tangier, painting by Henri Matisse, 1912. Pushkin Museum, Moscow. Photo: Arts Council

30 Wilhelm II as Crusader; cartoon from *L'Assiette au Beurre*, Paris, 1902. Photo: Freeman

31 Buffet-car, Usambara Railway, German East Africa. Photo: Ullstein Bilderdienst, Berlin

32 State monopoly of tobacco; cartoon from *Kladderadatsch*, Berlin, 1878. Photo: Freeman

33 Bismarck and the protective tariffs; cartoon from *Kladderadatsch*, Berlin, 1879. Photo: Freeman

34 Britain's Free Trade Policy; cartoon from Tariff Reform League pamphlet, 1903. Photo: Freeman

35 'Pears' Soap is the Best'; advertisement in the *Illustrated London News*, 1887. Photo: Freeman

36 Walter Rathenau. Photo: Ullstein Bilderdienst, Berlin

37 Viscount Haldane, drawing by R. Gould. National Portrait Gallery

38 Lord Cromer. Photo: Radio Times Hulton Picture Library

39 Wilhelm II with the shipbuilder Albert Ballin. Photo: Ullstein Bilderdienst, Berlin

40 Ferdinand de Lesseps with friends in Alexandria, 1865. Photo: Radio Times Hulton Picture Library

41 The Trans-Siberian Railway, 1911. Photo: Radio Times Hulton Picture Library

42 The launching of S.S. *Imperator*, 1912; postcard. Altonaer Museum, Hamburg

43 Wilhelm II visiting the Krupp works on its centenary. Photo: Ullstein Bilderdienst, Berlin

44 Cartoon criticizing Bismarck. *Kladderadatsch*, Berlin, 1884. Photo: Freeman

45 Cartoon reminding Britain of her social problems. *Fun*, 1875. Photo: Freeman

46 King Leopold II of the Belgians. *Der Berliner*, 1887. Photo: Freeman

47 Emperor Francis Joseph at the Ball of Industrialists, Budapest, 1902. From Max Herzig, *Kaiser Galerie*, 1908. Photo: Freeman

48 Post Office workers in Berlin. From *Berlin: Typen und Bilder*, Fischer Verlag, 1895. Photo: Freeman

49 Lord and Lady Curzon with Indian notables. Photo: Radio Times Hulton Picture Library

50 Cartoon on introduction of compulsory military service in France. *Figaro*, Vienna, 1867. Photo: Freeman

51 The prestige of the armed forces; advertisement in *Navy League Guide*, 1909. Photo: Freeman

52 'In Memoriam of Lord Kitchener'; postcard. British Museum. Photo: Freeman

53 Children in sailor-suits. Photo: The Mansell Collection, London

54 Edward VIII as a child wearing a sailor-suit. Photo: The Mansell Collection, London

55 Kaiser Wilhelm II and his reign, postcard, 1913. Altonaer Museum, Hamburg

56 Motto of the German National Shop Assistants' Association, 1899. Altonaer Museum, Hamburg

57 Thomas Carlyle, portrait by John Millais. National Portrait Gallery

58 'The New African Mission'; cartoon from *Fun*, 1875. Photo: Freeman

59 Vignette of the Navy League, 1898. British Museum. Photo: Freeman

60 Viscount Milner, portrait, 1901. National Portrait Gallery

61 Souvenir of Trafalgar, 1905. British Museum. Photo: Freeman

62 Wilhelm II's journey to Jerusalem; cartoon from *Le Rire*, 1898. Photo: Freeman

63 Emperor Francis Joseph's Jubilee celebration. Poster, Vienna, 1908. Historisches Museum, Vienna. Photo: R. Stepanek

64 Gabriel Hanotaux. Photo: H. Roger Viollet, Paris

65 Joseph Chamberlain, portrait by J. S. Sargent. National Portrait Gallery

66 Admiral von Tirpitz. Photo: Ullstein Bilderdienst, Berlin

67 French anti-colonial cartoon from *L'Assiette au Beurre*, Paris, 1902. Photo: Freeman

68 Cecil Rhodes: Monument of the Boer War; cartoon from *L'Assiette au Beurre*, Paris, 1902. Photo: Freeman

69 The Rhodes Memorial, Cape Town. Detail. Photo: J. Allan Cash, London

70 Benjamin Disraeli, portrait by John Millais. National Portrait Gallery

71 M.M. Muraviev, engraved portrait, 1866. Photo: Freeman

72 The Amur River. Illustration from Ukhtomsky's *Travels in the East of Nicholas II*, 1876. Photo: Freeman

73 Theodore Roosevelt 'civilizing' Cuba and the Philippines; cartoon from *L'Assiette au Beurre*, 1902. Photo: Freeman

74 Alberich, guardian of the treasure of the Nibelungen. From a production of Wagner's *The Ring of the Nibelungen*, Bayreuth, 1876. Photo: Theater-Museum, Munich

75 Campaign for eight-hour working day. Magazine cover, May Day 1906. *L'Assiette au Beurre*. Photo: Freeman

76 'The Strikers'. Illustration from *L'Assiette au Beurre*, 1904. Photo: Freeman

77 'The Achieving of the Sangreal'. Illustration by Aubrey Beardsley to *Le Mort d'Arthur*, 1894. Photo: Freeman

78 Alfred Tennyson, portrait by G. Watts, 1873. National Portrait Gallery

79 Rudyard Kipling, bust by G. Bingguely-Lejeune; 1936–37. National Portrait Gallery

80 Ernest Psichari. Photo: H. Roger Viollet, Paris

81 Monument of Commandant Marchand, Paris. Photo: H. Roger Viollet

82 The Albert Memorial, London. Photo: J. Allan Cash

83 The Albert Memorial, London. Detail: Europe. Photo: J. Allan Cash

84 The Albert Memorial, London. Detail: Africa. Photo: J. Allan Cash

85 General Gordon's statue, Khartoum. Photo: Radio Times Hulton Picture Library

86 The Bismarck Monument, Hamburg. Photo: Ullstein Bilderdienst, Berlin

87 Cecil Rhodes sepulchre, Matabele Mountains, Rhodesia. Photo: J. Allan Cash

88 The Rhodes Memorial, Cape Town. Photo J. Allan Cash

89 New Delhi, buildings by Sir Edwin Lutyens Photo: J. Allan Cash

90 Calcutta, the Victoria Memorial. Photo J. Allan Cash

91 Paris, the Musée des Colonies. Photo: H Roger Viollet

92 Friedrich Nietzsche, portrait by H. Olde Photo: Thames & Hudson archive

93 *Japanese Women*, pen and Chinese ink drawing by Emil Nolde. Nolde-Foundation, Seebul, Germany

94 *Three Siberians*, pen and ink drawing by Emil Nolde. Nolde-Foundation, Seebul, Germany

95 *South Sea Islander*, watercolour and Chinese ink drawing by Emil Nolde. Nolde-Foundation, Seebul, Germany

96 Obverse of H.M. Stanley medal commemorating the Emin Pasha Relief Expedition. Photo: Royal Geographical Society

97 Reverse of H.M. Stanley medal commemorating the Emin Pasha Relief Expedition. Photo Royal Geographical Society

98 'Polo under Difficulties', drawing by Robert Baden-Powell, *c.* 1880. British Museum Photo: Freeman

99 The British Officer in India, *c.* 1870. Photo Radio Times Hulton Picture Library

100 The '1000 Years of Russia' Monument Novgorod. Photo: Novosti Press Agency

101 Sarah Bernhardt as Joan of Arc; poster by E. S. Grasset, 1894. Victoria and Albert Museum. Photo: Freeman

102 'The White Peril'; cartoon from *L'Assiette au Beurre*, 1904. Photo: Freeman

103 'The Yellow Peril'; cartoon from *L'Assiette au Beurre*, 1904. Photo: Freeman

104 *The War*, painting by Arnold Böcklin, 1896 Dresden Galerie

105 'LES DEUX ¥EMPIRES'; French postcard 1914. British Museum. Photo: Freeman

106 'Any More to Come?' British postcard, 1914 British Museum. Photo: Freeman

107 The Kaiser as Satan II; British postcard, 1917 British Museum. Photo: Freeman

108 'Gott strafe England'; German postcard, 1916 Altonaer Museum, Hamburg

INDEX

References in italics denote illustration numbers

Address to the Serbs from Moscow (Chomyakov), 46
Adowa, 94
AEG, 27
Afghanistan, 34, 38
Africa, 34, 39, 56, 77, 176, 188; *31*; *see also* Congo; Egypt; South Africa; Sudan
Agadir Incident, 77
Agriculture, 27, 28, 30
Air forces, 98
Aircraft, 26, 92; *11*
Airship, dirigible, 26
Albert Memorial, London, *82-4*
Alexander II, Tsar, 45
Algeria, 67, 100, 105, 143; *28*
Alldeutscher Verband, 102, 106, 131
Alsace-Lorraine, 54
Amery, Leopold S., *156*
Ammonia production, 26
Amur territory, 127; *72*
Anglo-Indian Association, 100
Anglo-Persian (-Iranian) Oil Co., 78
Anglo-Saxon superiority, concept of, 51–2; *73*
Anti-colonialism, 117–24; *67*
Anti-Jamaica Committee, 102
Anzer, Bishop John Baptist, 104
Architecture, 147–52
Arendt, Hannah, 74, 192–3
Aristocracy, and new industrial *haute bourgeoisie*, 81–2; survival of, 84
Armaments, 30, 71–2, 190
Ashley, Sir William J., 134
'Asianism', 49
Asquith, Herbert H. (Earl of Oxford and Asquith), 78, 129, 133, 155
L'Assiette du Beurre, cartoons from, *11*, *15*, *18*, *30*, *67*, *68*, *73*, *75*, *76*, *102*, *103*
Associations, special purpose; *see* Pressure groups
Au Congo Belge (Mille), 144
Austin, Alfred, 142

Austria-Hungary, 12, 32, 33, 46, 47, 58–60, 94; *47*, *63*
Automobile, 26, 27; *10*

Baden-Powell, Robert, *98*
Baghdad Railway, 39, 70, 78
Bakunin, Mikhail, 128
Ballin, Albert, 67, 68; *39*
Bankers, in affairs of state, 65–7
Banks, as instruments of state policy, 70; favoured by state policies, 76
Banque de Paris et des Pays-Bas, 79
Banque de l'Union Parisienne, 79
Baring Bros. Bank, 66
Barrack Room Ballads (Kipling), 142
Beaconsfield, Earl of; *see* Disraeli
Beardsley, Aubrey, 77
Belgium, 54, 78, 104; *46*; *see also* Congo
Bell & Gray telephone, 24
Benz, Carl, 26
Berlin, growth in its importance, 31; Friedrichstrasse Railway Station, *7*; Post Office workers, *48*
Bernhardi, Gen. Friedrich von, 93
Bernhardt, Sarah, *101*
Bertrand, Louis, 143
Bessemer, Sir Henry, 26
Bicycle, 27; *9*
Birth control, 23
Bismarck, Prince Otto von, 16, 18, 31–4, 39, 69–70, 94–5, 113, 136, 138, 169; *12*, *33*, *44*, *86*
Bland, O.B., 172
Blatchford, Robert, 134, 139
Bloch, Johann von, 123
'Blue Water School', 96
Blunt, Wilfrid Scawen, 123
Böcklin, Arnold, *104*
Boers, 121, 123; *68*; *see also* South Africa
Bosanquet, Bernard, 154
Boulanger, Gen. Georges, 94
Bradley, Herbert, 154
Brailsford, H.N., 121
'Bricks and Mortar School', 96

Britain and the British Seas (Mackinder), 163
British Empire League, 105
British Government in India (Lord Curzon), 167
Brooke, Rajah, 141
Brunschwig, Henri, 77
Bukharin, Nikolai, 122
Bulb, electric light, 24
Bülow, Bernhard von, 113
Bureaucracy, 85, 87–90
Bulgarians, 102

Caird, Edward, 154, 155
Calcutta, Victoria Memorial, *90*
Cameroons, 39
Canada, 50, 54
Canning (food), 28
Cape Town, Rhodes Memorial, *69*, *88*
Carlyle, Thomas, 52, 101, 102, 133, 141, 154, 156, 166; *57*
Carnegie, Andrew, 81
Casement, Sir Roger, 123
Cassell, Sir Ernest, 67
Catholic Church, and imperialism, 104, 111
Chamberlain, Austen, 133
Chamberlain, Houston S., *157*
Chamberlain, Joseph, 15, 62, 66, 112, 115, 129, 133, 136; *65*
Chemical industry, advances in, nineteenth century, 26; relation to government, 72
Chernayev, Gen. Mikhail, 94
China, 36, 49, 71, 76, 77, 104, 127
Chomyakov, A.S., 44, 46, 101
Church, decline in authority of, 9; attitude of to imperialism, 52, 104, 108, 111; *see also* Missionary societies
Churchill, Sir Winston S., 78
Cinematograph, 28
Class, Heinrich, 131
Class war, 18, 76, 137–9, 158, 193
Colonial Conferences, 110
Colonialism, difference from imperialism, 64
Colonies, Colonial Policies and Emigration (Roscher), 103

Colonization and the Making of Mankind (Lüthy), 195
Colons, 100
Coloured labour, opposition to, 83; see also 'Yellow Peril'
Coloured troops, interest aroused by, 94
Comité de l'Afrique Française, 106
Commonwealth, development of concept of, 54
Communications, development of, 24, 26–8
Compromises, international, pre-First World War, 38–9
Congo, 78, 104, 123, 144
Conscription, 106–7; 50
Corradini, Enrico, 114
Courtney, 1st Baron, 121
Cramb, J.A., 160–1, 171, 179
Cromer, 1st Earl of, 66; 38
Cunningham, William, 134
Curie, Marie and Pierre, 26
Curtis, Lionel, 54, 156
Curzon, Lord, 53, 151, 167, 170, 181; 49
Cyril (Drage), 141

Daimler, Gottlieb, 26
Dalhousie, Marquess, 167
Danilevsky, N.Y., 45, 157, 160, 171; 22
Dehmel, Richard, 68
Delbrück, Hans, 161
Democracy, and imperialism, 125–36
Democracy and Reaction (Hobhouse), 118–19, 156
Demokratie und Kaisertum (Naumann), 140
Dernburg, Bernhard, 66, 131
Der deutsche Gedanke in der Welt, 60
Deutsche Kolonialgesellschaft, 106
Deutscher Nationalverein, 107
Diesel, Rudolf, 26
Dilke, Sir Charles, 50–1, 129, 133, 171, 180; 25
Dilthey, Wilhelm, 158
Disraeli, Benjamin, 54, 114, 125, 126, 141; 70
Dmovsky, Roman, 47
Dobell, Sidney, 141
Dostoyevsky, Fyodor, 48, 49
Douwes-Dekker, Ed., 123
Drage, Geoffrey, 52, 141
Drake, an English Epic (Noyes), 142

Dreikaiserbund (League of the Three Emperors), 32
Du Rôle social de l'officier (Lyautey), 92, 167
'Dual Mandate' concept, 53
Duncan, Patrick, 156
Dunlop, J.B., 26
Durham, Lord, 128
Dyestuffs, synthetic, 26
Dynamite, 26
Dynamo, 24

Eastern Question, 47–9
Edison, T.A., 24
Edward VII, 67
Edward VIII, 54
Egypt, 38, 66, 76, 123; 14, 23, 40
Electric vehicles, 24, 27, 28
Electrotechnics, 24, 26, 72
Emigration, from Europe, 22
Emin Pasha Relief Expedition medal, 96, 97
Empire Economic Union, 107
England's Day: A War Saga (Dobell), 141
Etienne, Eugène N., 115, 126
Eucken, Rudolf, 157
Exhibitions, 108
The Expansion of England (Seeley), 160
Exporting and the imperialist economy, 64, 79
Eyre, Edward John, Governor of Jamaica, 102

Fabian Society, 134
Fabre, Ferdinand, 146
Fabry, Frederic, 104
Fadeyev, General, 48, 94
Farrière, Claude, 146
Fashoda Crisis, 35
Federal Union Committee, 106
Ferry, Jules, 77, 114, 124, 126
Figaro, cartoons from, 4, 21, 50
First World War, causes of, 38–40, 182; propaganda, 52, 105–8; significance of, 183 ff.
Flandrin, Hippolyte, 27
Flottenverein, 98, 106
Forster, W.E., 129
Foster, R.A., 19
France, 10, 16, 18, 31, 34, 35, 37, 54–7, 66, 70, 77, 78–9, 84, 94, 96, 102, 103, 104, 106, 111, 112, 123, 124, 126, 129, 143–5, 158, 161, 170, 187, 188; 5, 9, 10, 11, 18, 27–9, 40, 50, 64, 67, 68, 75, 76, 80, 81, 91, 101–3, 106

Francis Joseph, Emperor of Austria, 47, 63
Franco-Russian Alliance, 37; 17
Free trade, 14, 61–3, 117, 122, 133, 137, 190; 34
Frenssen, Gustav, 145
Frere, Sir Bartle, 142
Friedjung, Heinrich, 13
Froude, James, 51, 102; 26
Fun, cartoons from, 45, 58
Furness, H., 25

Gallieni, Gen. Joseph Simon, 94
Gambetta, Léon, 129
Gandy, J.M., 1, 2
The Geographical Pivot of History (Mackinder), 163
Geographical societies, 102–4, 161; 96–7
Geography, 161–4
Geopolitics, 163–4
German National Shop Assistants' Association, 56
The German Panic (Hobson), 174
Germany, 16, 18, 31–4, 36, 37, 38, 39, 58–60, 66–7, 69–72, 77, 79, 84, 85, 94–8, 102, 103, 104, 106, 107, 111, 113, 114, 115, 116, 123, 126, 130–5, 138–40, 145, 156, 157, 158, 161, 164, 169, 170, 179, 184–5, 188; 5, 7, 12, 13, 30–3, 36, 39, 43, 44, 48, 55, 56, 62, 66, 74, 86, 92–5, 104, 108
Giddings, F.H., 157, 158
Gilchrist, Percy, 27
Giolitti, Giovanni, 114
Gladstone, W.E., 15, 114
Gobineau, Count Arthur, 157
Godeffroy, Messrs, 70
Goldie, George Taubmann, 80
Goltz, Field-Marshal Freiherr Colmar von der, 93
Gordon, Gen. Charles, 94; 85
Goulding, E., 138
Gramophone, 28
La grande route de Tschad (Lenfant), 143
Great Britain, 10, 14, 15, 33, 34, 35, 36, 38, 50–4, 56, 66, 67, 76, 77, 78, 80, 84, 85, 89, 96, 97, 101, 102 ff., 110 ff., 121, 123, 128–30, 133–8, 141–3, 154–6, 158, 160, 161, 167–8, 170, 179, 180–1, 188; 1, 2, 4, 6, 14, 16, 19, 25, 26, 34, 35, 37, 38, 45, 49, 51–4, 57–61, 65, 68–70, 77–9, 82–5, 87–90, 96–9, 101, 105, 107
Great Exhibition (1851), 108

Great Powers (Kjellén), 164
Great War; see First World War
Greater Britain . . . (Dilke), 50,
129, 171
Green, T.H., 154
Grégorie, Bishop, 123
Grey of Fallodon, Viscount, 129,
133, 155, 179
Grimm, Hans, 145, 151
Gumplowicz, Ludwig, 157

Haber-Bosch process, 26
Habsburg Empire; see Austria-
Hungary
Haeckel, Ernst, 157
Hague Conferences, 123
Haldane, Viscount, 67, 129, 133,
155; 37
Hamburg, Bismarck Monument,
68; 86
Hanotaux, Gabriel, 115, 126; 64
'Harbour Festival' (Dehmel), 68
Haushofer, Karl, 163, 164
Haute bourgeoisie, status of, 81-2
Hedin, Sven, 163
'Heimatkunst', 145, 151
Henri d'Orléans, Prince, 126
Heredity, establishment of rules
of, 26
Hertz, H., 24
Herzen, Alexander, 128
Hilferding, Rudolf, 122
History, 159-61, 170-1
Hobhouse, Emily, 113
Hobhouse, Leonard T., 118-19,
120, 121, 122, 156, 158
Hobson, J.A., 79, 117, 120, 134,
174, 189-91, 193
Hugenberg, Alfred, 67, 131
Hydroelectric generating station,
first, 26

Idealism, 156
Idylls of the King (Tennyson), 77
I. G. Farben trust, 27
Ignatiev, Count, 115
S.S. Imperator, 72; 42
Imperial Chemical Industries Ltd,
27
Imperial Conferences, 110
Imperial Federation League, 105,
129, 138
Imperial Institute, 106
Imperialism (Hobson), 117, 189-
91
Imperialism, British concept of,
50-4; economic aspects of, 61-

83; expansionism as a key factor
in, 15; French concept of, 54-7;
German concept of, 58-60; his-
tory of term, 10; ideology of,
11-13; industrialization of rela-
tion to, 71-3; middle class
support of, 69, 86; strategic
considerations of, 12
Imperialism, the Highest Stage of
Capitalism (Lenin), 61, 191
Imperium et libertas concept, 125,
129, 130
India, 14, 50, 76, 80, 89, 100, 123,
141, 151, 167-8, 180-1, 189; 49,
89, 90, 99
Indo-China, 34
Internal combustion engine, 26
International Nickel Co., 27
Internationalism, 42, 123
Ireland, 112
'Island Kingdom', British con-
cept of, 52
Italy, 31, 33, 34, 36, 67, 84, 107,
114, 158, 170, 187-8

Jamaica Committee, 102
Jameson Raid, 142
Jannasch, Robert, 103
Japan, 31, 34, 36, 76, 175, 188; 15,
16
Japanese women (Nolde), 93
Jerusalem, 111; 62
'Jeune Ecole', 96
Jews, 85, 176
Joan of Arc, 101
Jonnart, Charles C., 66
Journalism, 86-7, 108, 123, 160;
special pleading for military, 93
Jubilees, 110

'Kathedersozialisten', 134
Katkov, M.N., 86
Kautsky, Karl, 122, 192
Khartoum, Fall of (1885), 94;
Gordon Statue, 85
Kidd, Benjamin, 157, 158
Kim (Kipling), 141
Kingsley, Charles, 101, 141, 179
Kipling, Rudyard, 51, 141, 142,
144, 179; 79
Kitchener, Field-Marshal Earl,
94; 52
Kjellén, Rudolf, 163, 164
Kladderadatsch, cartoons from, 12,
13, 32, 33, 44
Krupp, house and firm of, 67, 71,
72, 81; 43

Lafitte, Jacques, 66
Lapouge, Count Vacher de, 157
Lassalle, Ferdinand, 140
Latin America, 36, 76
Lavigerie, Cardinal Charles Mar-
tial, 104-5
'League of the Three Emperors',
32
Lebensphilosophie, 158-9, 179
Legon, University of, 151
Lenfant, Commander, 143
Lenin, V.I., 61, 122, 191
Lenz, Max, 161
Leopold II, King of the Belgians,
72, 104, 144; 46
Leroy-Beaulieu, Anatole, 102
Lesseps, Ferdinand de, 40
Lettow-Vorbeck, Paul von, 94
Liberal-Unionist party, 112
Liga für Menschenrechte, 122
Linde, Carl von, 26
Liquefaction of air, 26
Literature, 141-7
Locomotive, electric, 24
London, buildings and monu-
ments in, 1, 2, 6, 82-4
London School of Economics,
120, 163
Lothian, Lord (Philip Kerr), 156
Lotze, Rudolf H., 155
Louis-Philippe, King of France,
10
Lugard, Lord, 53
Lukács, Georg, 158
Lüthy, H., 195
Lutyens, Sir Edwin, 151; 89
Luxemburg, Rosa, 122, 191
Lyautey, Marshal Louis Hubert,
92, 93, 94, 126, 151, 166-8

Machine-gun, 30, 92
Mackinder, John Halford, 133,
163-4
Mackinnon, William, 80
Mahan, Admiral Alfred T., 96
Malthusianism, 23
Manchester School, 62, 64, 118,
128
Manchuria, 49
Manchurian Railway, 70
Marchaud, Commandant Jean-
Baptiste, 81
Marcks, Erich, 161
Marconi, Guglielmo, 24
Martin brothers, 27
Marxism, 122, 134, 137, 191-2
Matisse, Henri, 29
Maupassant, Guy de, 146

Max Havelaar (Douwes-Dekker), 123
Maybach, Wilhelm, 26
Medicine, nineteenth century advance in, 27
Mediterranean Treaty (1887), 33
Melchett, Lord, 27
Memoir of Hubert Hervey . . . (Grey), 179
Mendel, G.J., 26
Mendizabal, Juan Alvarez y, 66
Middle class, industrial, 82; professional, 85–6, 110
Military, educational role of, 91–2; role of in imperialism, 90–8, 139–40, 178–9; *50, 51*
Millais, Sir John E., *57*
Mille, Pierre, 144
Milner, Viscount, 107, 139, 155; *60*
Ministerial support of imperialism, 115
Missionary societies, 104–5; *58*
Moissan, Henri, 26
Moltke, Field-Marshal Helmuth von, 178
Mond, Ludwig, 26, 27
Montenegro, 108
Morocco, 38, 39; *18*
'Multatuli', 123, 146
Muraviev-Amursky, General, 127–8; *71*
Musée de la France d'Outre Mer (Musée des Colonies), 151, 170; *91*
Mussolini, Benito, 187–8
Mutation, 26

Napoleon III, 10, 16, 56, 133; *27*
Narodnost, concept of, 44
The Nation's Awakening (Wilkinson), 155
National Service League, 106–7
National Social Catechism (Naumann), 139–40
National socialism, 131–2, 138–40
Nationalism, as source of imperialism, 41–2, 131, 180, 193; as source of opposition, 124
Nationalsozialer Verein, 131–2, 139
Naumann, Friedrich, 114, 131–2, 139–40
Navies and imperialism, 96–8; *53, 54, 61*
Navy League, 98, 106; *51, 59*
Navy Records Society, 106
Necker, Jacques, 66

Neo-mercantilism, 63, 77, 118
Neo-Slavism, 46–7, 128
Netherlands, 36
New Delhi, 151; *89*
'New Idealism', 154–6, 160, 179
Nicholas I, Tsar, 15
Nicholas II, Tsar, 15
Nickel manufacture, 26
Nietzsche, Friedrich, 158, 159; *52*
Nobel, Alfred, 26, 123
Nolde, Emil, *93–5*
Northcliffe, Viscount, 86
La Nouvelle France (Prévost-Paradol), 171
Novgorod, '1000 Years of Russia' Monument, *100*
Noyes, Alfred, 142
Nutrition, changes in, 28, 30
Nye Committee, 76

Oath at Versailles, 5
Oceana or England and her Colonies (Froude), 51
Octobrists, 114
'Ode to the Slavs' (Chomyakov), 44
Officer corps, 90, 110
Olde, H., *92*
Opinion on the Eastern Question (Fadeyev), 47
Opium War, 76
'Oriental Question', 47–9
The Origin and Destiny of Imperial Britain (Cramb), 160–1, 171
Orthodox Church, 104, 108, 111
Otto, Nicolas, 26
Ottoman Empire; *see* Turkey
Oxford and Asquith, Earl of; *see* Asquith
Oxford University, and the 'New Idealism', 154–6, 160

Pacifism, 42, 93, 123
Palace design (Gandy), *1*
Palmerston, 3rd Viscount, 52
'Pan'-movements, 42, 54–5, 106, 107, 116, 129
Pan-Slavism, 14, 44–50, 94, 101, 102, 107, 108, 114, 126, 128, 160, 170, 180; *21*
Paris, Musée de la France d'Outre Mer, 151, 170; *91*
Parking, George R., 138
Parliament, Houses of, design by Gandy, *2*
Parliamentary imperialist groups, 111–13

Paternalism of entrepreneurs, 74–5
Pears soap advertisement, *35*
Pearson, Karl, 157
Peel, Sir Robert, 66
Peking, Treaty of, 127
Perier, Casimir, 66
Le Péril Financier, 174
Le Péril National, 174
Persia, 34, 38, 104
Peter Moors Fahrt nach Südwest (Frenssen), 145
Peters, Carl, 102, 141
Petroleum interests, rivalry between, 76
Philosophy, 154–9
Pictures for Little Englanders, 19
Plastic arts, 147–52
Pogodin, M.P., 44, 101, 160
Poland, 47
Politische Geographie (Ratzel), 163
'Polo under difficulties', *98*
Population, European increase nineteenth century, 19–20, 22–3; problems, 172, 190
Portugal, overseas possessions of, 36, 39
Positivism, 157
Power, cult of, 168–9
Power plant, first electric, 24
Press, 86–7, 93, 108; *see also* Journalism
Pressure groups, 96, 99–100, 102–8, 116
Prévost-Paradol, Lucien, 56, 143, 171
Primrose League, 105, 125
Prinetti, Giulio, 67
Propaganda, 184; *see also* Journalism; Press; Pressure groups
Protection (economic), 62, 106, 133, 136, 164; *33*
Protection of Aborigines Society, 122
Protestantism and imperialism, 52, 104, 111
'Protocols of the Elders of Zion', 176
'Prussian virtues', 166
Psichari, Ernest, 143–4; *80*
Pushkin, Alexander, 44
Putilov, 71

Quinet, Edgar, 55

Racialism, 157, 172
Radium, discovery of, 26

214

Railways, 27, 28, 39, 70–1, 78; 7, 8, *31*, *41*
Rambaud, Alfred, 102
Ranke, Leopold von, and 'Ranke Renaissance' group, 157, 161
Rathenau, Walter, 66, 81; *36*
Ratzel, Friedrich, 163
Ratzenhofer, Gustav, 157
Reactionaries, opposition of to imperialism, 126
Reform; *see* Social reform
Refrigeration, 28
Reis telephone, 24
Remembrance days, 108
Rhodes, Cecil, 51, 80, 81, 86, 136, 141, 142; *68*, *69*, *87*, *88*
The Ring (Wagner), 74
Le Rire, cartoon from, *62*
Roberts, Field-Marshal Earl, 93, 94, 107
Rockefeller, John D., 81
Rohrbach, Paul, 60, 180
Roosevelt, President Theodore, 129; *73*
Roscher, Wilhelm, 103
Rosebery, Lord, 41, 114, 129, 133, 164
Rostow, W. W., 61
Round Table, 107
Royal Colonial Society (later Institute), 103, 106
Royal Dutch Shell, 78
Royal Exchange, London, *6*
Rumania, 33
Russia, 14, 15, 32, 33, 34, 36, 38, 43–50, 70, 76, 78–9, 84, 97, 101, 102, 107, 108, 111, 114, 115, 123, 126, 127, 145, 158, 174–5, 188; *3*, *4*, *15*, *17*, *20–4*, *41*, *71*, *72*, *100*
Russia and Europe (Danilevsky), 45, 160, 171; *22*
Russian-Chinese Bank, 79
Russian Revolution, 185
Russo-Asiatic Musings (Ukhtomsky), 171
Russo-Japanese conflict, *15*, *16*

Saint-Etienne steelworks, 66
Salisbury, 3rd Marquess of, 124
Samoa Crisis, 39, 70
Sargent, J.S., *65*
Sarraut, Albert, 126
Schäfer, Dietrich, 161
Scheler, Max, 158
Schneider-Creuzot works, 71
Schoelcher, Viktor, 123

Schumpeter, Joseph A., 192, 193
Science and the 'Scientific Revolution', 23 ff., 153, 183
Seeley, J. R., 160, 171
Service, ethos of, 165–8
Shipping lines, 70; *42*
Siegfried, André, 102
Siemens, Werner, 24, 27
Skobelev, Gen. Mikhail, 94
Skoda, 71
Slav Congress (1848), 45; (1867) 45, 108
Slav-Ethnographic Exhibition, 108
Slavische Blätter, 20
Slavophile movement, 43–50
Social Darwinism, 13, 52, 60, 120, 157–8, 179
Social imperialism; *see below* Social reform
Social reform, 133–40
Socialism, 121–2, 133 ff., 176; military opposition to, 93; *see also* Class war
Società Nationale, 107
Société des Ecrivains et Romanciers Coloniaux, 144
Société Générale, 79
Société de Géographie Commerciale, 103
Soda, 26
Soloviev, Vladimir, 49, 145
Sombart, Werner, 60
South Africa, 77, 155; *69*, *88*; *see also* Boers
South Sea Islander (Nolde), *94*
Spain, 12, 39, 66, 188
Spanish-American War (1898), 35
Spencer, Herbert, 121
Spengler, Oswald, 158, 161
The Stages of Economic Growth . . . (Rostow), 61
Stalin, Josef, 188
Stanley, H. M., *96*, *97*
The State as Life-Form (Kjellén), 164
Stead, W. T., 86, 136
Steel production, 26
Stein, Laurenz von, 140
Stowe, Harriet Beecher, 123
Submarines, 30, 92
Sudan, 35, 94; *85*
Suez Canal Co., 66, 69, 78
Suttner, Berta von, 123
Sweden, 163, 164
Swinburne, Algernon, 142
Synthetics, 28

Tangier, *29*
Tank, 30
Tariff Reform League, 106, 136; *34*
Technological advance, 24–30, 153–4, 183
Telephone, 24, 28
Tennyson, Alfred, Lord, 102, 142, 179; *78*
Terres de Soleil et de Sommeil (Psichari), 143–4
Thackeray, William M., 167
Thomas, J. G., 27
'Thousand Years of Russia' Monument, *100*
Three Siberians (Nolde), *94*
Tibet, 38
Tirpitz, Grand Admiral Alfred von, 98, 115; *66*
Tonkin, 77
Toynbee, Arnold, 155
Trade Unions, 122; *56*, *75*, *76*
Trafalgar souvenir, *61*
Tram, 27
Transport, 26, 27–8, 153; *7–11*, *31*, *41–2*
Trans-Sahara Railway project, 71
Trans-Siberian Railway, 70; *41*
Travels in the East of Nicholas II (Ukhtomsky), *3*, *23*, *72*
Triple Alliance, 33, 37, 70; *13*
Triple Entente, 38, 70
'Trusteeship' concept, 50
Tunis, 77
Turkey, 12, 14, 34, 47–8, 70, 71, 102, 188
Typewriter, invention of, 30
Tyre, pneumatic, 26
Tyuchev, F. J., 44, 101

Ukhtomsky, Count Esper, 49, 171; *3*, *23*, *72*
Uncle Tom's Cabin (Stowe), 123
Union Minière du Haute Katanga, 78
United Empire Trade League, 106
United States, 22, 31, 34, 35, 38, 76, 96, 128, 174, 188; *73*
Urbanization, 20
Usambara Railway, buffet car, *31*
Ussuri, 49, 127

Verein für das Deutschtum im Ausland, 107
Verein für Handelsgeographie und Förderung deutsches Interessen im Ausland, 103

Verein für Sozialpolitik, 134
Veuillot, Louis, 104
Vickers-Armstrong, 71
Victoria, Queen, 114; *19*
Vitalism, 178–9
Vladivostok, 49; *24*
Vogüe, Vicomte de, 174
Volk ohne Raum (Grimm), 145
Volkstum, concept of, 44, 58
Vostokniki, 48–9
Vries, Hugo de, 26

Die Waffen Nieder (Suttner), 123
Wagner, Adolf, 134
Wakefield, Gibbon, 128
Wallace, William, 154
Walloons, 54
War, as an element of imperialist policy, 178–9; *104*
War of 1914–18; *see* First World War

Wartenburg, Col. Graf Maximilian Yorck von, 161
Watts, G.F., *78*
Weber, Max, 131, 134, 169
Wehrverein, 106
Welfare of industrial workers, 74–6
Weltgeschichte in Umrissen (Wartenburg), 161
Werner, Anton von, 5
Westward Ho! (Kingsley), 141
'White Man's Burden, The', (Kipling), 51, 142
Wilberforce, William, 123
Wilde, Oscar, 142
Wilhelm II, Kaiser, 16, 67, 68, 72, 97, 111, 114, 132, 140; *30, 39, 43, 55, 62*
Wilkinson, Spenser, 155
Wilson, President Woodrow, 185, 188
Wireless telegraphy, 24, 28

Wirth, A., 172
Witte, Count Sergei, 124
Woltmann, Ludwig, 157
Women, emancipation of, 9, 85
Wordsworth, William, 156
Working class, emancipation of, 9; welfare of, 74–6; consolidation, 82; representation of, 137; *see also* Class war; Socialism
Wright brothers, 26

'Yellow Peril', 83, 145, 172, 175; *103*
Youth, emancipation of, 9

Zanzibar-Heligoland Agreement, 102
Zeppelinwerke, 71
Die Zerstorung der Vernunft (Lukács), 158
Zionism, 176